THE YEAR Y
WERE BOR

1951

A fascinating book about the year 1951 with information on:
Events of the year UK, Adverts of 1951, Cost of living, Births, Deaths, Sporting events,
Book publications, Movies, Music, World events and People in power.

Dewar's
"White Label"
SCOTCH WHISKY

INDEX

UK EVENTS OF 1951

January

1st The Archers is a British radio soap opera on BBC Radio 4—the BBC's main spoken-word channel— broadcast since 1951. It was initially billed an everyday story of country folk and now, a contemporary drama in a rural setting. Having aired over 19,000 episodes, it is the world's longest-running drama. Five pilot episodes were aired in 1950 and the first episode was broadcast nationally on the 1st January 1951. A significant show in British popular culture, and with over five million listeners, it is Radio 4's most listened-to non-news programme, and with over one million listeners via the internet, the programme holds the record for BBC Radio online listening figures. In February 2019, a panel of 46 broadcasting industry experts, of which 42 had a professional connection to the BBC, listed The Archers as the second-greatest radio programme of all time. Partly established with the aim towards educating farmers following World War II, The Archers soon became a popular source of entertainment for the population at large, attracting nine million listeners by 1953.

2nd The Ford Consul is a car that was manufactured by Ford UK from 1951 to 1962. Between 1951 and 1962, the Consul was the four-cylinder base model of the three-model Ford Zephyr range, comprising Consul, Zephyr, and Zephyr Zodiac. The 1500 cc four-cylinder Consul was first shown at the 1950 London Motor Show. It was the start of Ford of Britain's successful attack on the family saloon car market. With stablemate Zephyr, it was the first British Ford with modern unibody construction. The Zephyr Six replaced the larger-engine V-8 Pilot which had been made in only small numbers. It was also the first car they built with up-to-date technology. The new 1508 cc 47 bhp (35 kW) engine had overhead valves, and hydraulic clutch operation was used, which in 1950 was an unusual feature. However, a three-speed gearbox, with synchromesh only on second and top, was retained. The Consul was also the first British production car to use the now-common MacPherson strut independent front suspension.

January

4th British Board of Film Censors introduces X rating for films "Suitable for those aged 16 and over".

9th The government announces abandonment of the Tanganyika groundnut scheme, writing off £36,500,000. The Tanganyika groundnut scheme, or East Africa groundnut scheme, was a failed attempt by the British government to cultivate tracts of Tanganyika (modern-day Tanzania) with peanuts. Launched in the aftermath of World War II by the administration of prime minister Clement Attlee, the project was finally abandoned as unworkable in 1951 at considerable cost. The fact that the region's terrain and rainfall were totally inappropriate for growing groundnuts, as well as the project's ultimate cost and failure, led to the scheme being popularly seen as a symbol of government failure in late colonial Africa.

February

1st Ferranti deliver their first Mark 1 computer to the University of Manchester, the world's first commercially available general-purpose electronic computer. The Ferranti Mark 1, also known as the Manchester Electronic Computer in its sales literature, and thus sometimes called the Manchester Ferranti, was the world's first commercially available general-purpose electronic computer. It was "the tidied up and commercialised version of the Manchester computer". The first machine was delivered to the University of Manchester in February 1951 ahead of the UNIVAC I, which was sold to the United States Census Bureau on the 31st March 1951, although not delivered until late December the following year.

2nd Éamon de Valera visits Newry for the first time since his arrest there in 1924. Prior to de Valera's political career, he was a Commandant at Boland's Mill during the 1916 Easter Rising. He was arrested, sentenced to death but released for a variety of reasons, including the public response to the British execution of Rising leaders. He returned to Ireland after being jailed in England and became one of the leading political figures of the War of Independence. After the signing of the Anglo-Irish Treaty, de Valera served as the political leader of Anti-Treaty Sinn Féin until 1926, when he, along with many supporters, left the party to set up Fianna Fáil. From there, de Valera went on to be at the forefront of Irish politics until the turn of the 1960s. He took over as President of the Executive Council from W. T. Cosgrave and later Taoiseach, with the passing of the Constitution of Ireland in 1937. He served as Taoiseach on three different occasions; from 1937 to 1948, from 1951 to 1954 and finally from 1957 to 1959. He remains the longest serving Taoiseach by total days served in the post. He resigned in 1959 upon his election as President of Ireland.

21st | An English Electric Canberra (with Rolls-Royce Avon engines) becomes the first jet to make an unrefuelled Transatlantic flight, taking 4 hours 37 minutes from RAF Aldergrove in Northern Ireland to Gander in Newfoundland. The English Electric Canberra is a British first-generation jet-powered medium bomber. It was developed by English Electric during the mid-to-late 1940s in response to a 1944 Air Ministry requirement for a successor to the wartime de Havilland Mosquito fast bomber. Throughout most of the 1950s, the Canberra could fly at a higher altitude than any other aircraft in the world. In 1957, a Canberra established a world altitude record of 70,310 feet (21,430 m). In addition to being a tactical nuclear strike aircraft, the Canberra proved to be highly adaptable, serving in varied roles such as tactical bombing and photographic and electronic reconnaissance. Canberra's served in the Suez Crisis, the Vietnam War, the Falklands War, the Indo-Pakistani wars, and numerous African conflicts.

English Electric Canberra

22nd | Film noir Pool of London is released, the first British film with a major role for a black actor, Bermuda-born Earl Cameron. The story centres on the crew of the merchant ship Dunbar, which docks in the Pool of London. The crew members are given shore leave, and soon become involved in smuggling and petty crime in post-war London. The film is mainly known for portraying the first interracial relationship in a British film. "Pool of London" premiered at the Odeon Leicester Square in London on the 22nd February 1951.

March

13th | Pineapple Poll, a Gilbert and Sullivan-inspired comic ballet, created by choreographer John Cranko with arranger Sir Charles Mackerras, is premiered at Sadler's Wells Theatre by the Sadler's Wells Ballet.

17th | The Free Presbyterian Church of Ulster is a Christian denomination founded by Ian Paisley. The Free Presbyterian Church of Ulster began on the 17th March 1951 (St Patrick's Day) as the result of a conflict between some members of the local Lissara Presbyterian congregation in Crossgar, County Down, Northern Ireland, and the Down Presbytery of the Presbyterian Church in Ireland.

Dennis and Gnasher (previously titled Dennis the Menace and Gnasher, and originally titled Dennis the Menace) is a long-running comic strip in the British children's comic The Beano, published by DC Thomson, of Dundee, Scotland. The comic stars a boy named Dennis the Menace and his Abyssinian wire-haired tripe hound Gnasher. The strip first appeared in issue 452, dated 17th March 1951 and is the longest-running strip in the comic. The idea and name of the character emerged when the comic's editor heard a British music hall song with the chorus "I'm Dennis the Menace from Venice". The creation of Dennis in the 1950s saw sales of The Beano soar. From issue 1678 onwards (dated 14th September 1974) Dennis the Menace replaced Biffo the Bear on the front cover, and has been there ever since. Dennis the Menace and Gnasher was first drawn by David Law (1951–1970) who gave the mischievous boy his distinctive red and black striped jersey, outsized shoes and devilish grin.

April

11th The Stone of Scone is located in Forfar, having been stolen by Scottish nationalists. The Stone of Scone also known as the Stone of Destiny, and often referred to in England as The Coronation Stone—is an oblong block of red sandstone that has been used for centuries in the coronation of the monarchs of Scotland, and later also when the monarchs of Scotland became monarchs of England as well as in the coronations of the monarchs of Great Britain and latterly of the United Kingdom following the acts of union. Historically, the artefact was kept at the now-ruined Scone Abbey in Scone, near Perth, Scotland.

16th HMS Affray, a British Amphion-class submarine, was the last Royal Navy submarine to be lost at sea, on the 16th April 1951, with the loss of 75 lives. All vessels of her class were given names beginning with the letter A; she was the only ship of the Royal Navy to be named after a particularly noisy and disorderly fight. HMS Affray was built in the closing stages of the Second World War. She was one of 16 submarines of her class which were originally designed for use in the Pacific Ocean against Japan.

17th The Peak District is established as the first of the national parks of England and Wales. The Lake District is designated so in May, and designations of Snowdonia and Dartmoor come into effect on the 20th November.

19th The Attorney General for Northern Ireland, Ed Warnock, referring to the resignation of Noel Browne from the Government of the Republic of Ireland, says that Ireland is really ruled by Maynooth.

22nd Korean War: Battle of the Imjin River: the 29th Infantry Brigade of the British Army serving with the United Nations put up brave but ultimately unsuccessful resistance to the Chinese advance, with 141 UN troops killed. The last stand of the 1st Battalion, The Gloucestershire Regiment (the "Glorious Glosters") at Hill 235 rapidly becomes part of modern military tradition.

23rd Aneurin Bevan, recently appointed as Minister of Labour and National Service, together with John Freeman and Harold Wilson, resign from the government in protest at Hugh Gaitskell's announcement in the Budget on the 10th April to introduce prescription charges for dental care and spectacles (in order to meet the financial demands imposed by the Korean War).

April

28th | Newcastle United wins the FA Cup for the fourth time with a 2–0 win over Blackpool at Wembley Stadium. Jackie Milburn scores both goals in front of a crowd of 100,000 spectators.

May

3rd | George VI opens the Festival of Britain in London, including the Royal Festival Hall, Dome of Discovery and Skylon. This will be last major public event attended by the King and Queen together. Festival Gardens and a fun fair are opened in Battersea Park, and the Lansbury Estate in Poplar is begun this year as a housing showcase. The Festival of Britain was a national exhibition and fair that reached millions of visitors throughout the United Kingdom in the summer of 1951. Labour cabinet member Herbert Morrison was the prime mover; in 1947 he started with the original plan to celebrate the centennial of the Great Exhibition of 1851. However it was not to be another World Fair, for international themes were absent, as was the British Commonwealth. Instead the 1951 festival focused entirely on Britain and its achievements; it was funded chiefly by the government, with a budget of £12 million.

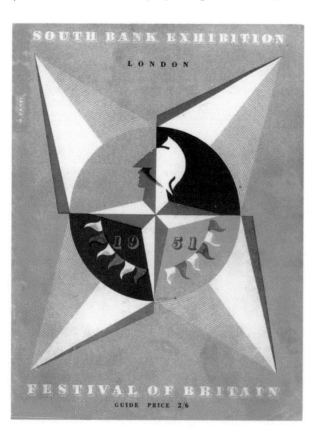 

3rd | Josef Herman's Miners, a mural commissioned for the Minerals of the Island Pavilion at the Festival of Britain, is displayed for the first time.

4th | Festival Ship Campania cruises the seaports. She was the Festival of Britain's exhibition ship, touring the country's ports with a civilian crew as the Festival Ship Campania to supplement the main exhibition in London and two thousand local events. Repainted white, the ship was decorated with skeleton masts and bunting. Officially named the Sea Travelling Exhibition, the exhibits were intended to reflect the main London Exhibition. Like the Festival's Land Travelling Exhibition, they were divided into three sections, the "Land of Britain", "Discovery" and "The People at Home".

May

14th | The Talyllyn Railway is reopened by the Talyllyn Railway Preservation Society, generally considered to be the world's first such voluntary body to operate a railway.

28th | The Goon Show was a British radio comedy programme, originally produced and broadcast by the BBC Home Service from 1951 to 1960, with occasional repeats on the BBC Light Programme. The first series, broadcast from the 28th May to 20th September 1951, was titled Crazy People; subsequent series had the title The Goon Show, a title inspired, according to Spike Milligan, by a Popeye character.

Princess Elizabeth opens the Exhibition of Industrial Power – the latest part of the Festival of Britain – in Glasgow.

29th | Guy Burgess and Donald Maclean defect to the Soviet Union. Were both British diplomat and Soviet agents and members of the Cambridge Five spy ring that operated from the mid-1930s to the early years of the Cold War era. There defection in 1951 to the Soviet Union led to a serious breach in Anglo-United States intelligence co-operation, and caused long-lasting disruption and demoralisation in Britain's foreign and diplomatic services.

June

2nd | Workington F.C. is elected to the Football League in place of New Brighton A.F.C., and will compete in the Football League Third Division North for the 1951-52 season.

26th | Ealing comedy film The Lavender Hill Mob released. The film won the Academy Award for Best Writing, Story and Screenplay. Guinness was nominated for the award of Best Actor in a Leading Role. The film also won the BAFTA Award for Best British Film.

July

1st | Public Order Act (Northern Ireland) 1951 is introduced, requiring organisers of public processions to give 48 hours' notice to the Royal Ulster Constabulary (RUC), except for funeral processions and "public processions which are customarily held along a particular route".

10th | Boxer Randy Turpin beats the American Sugar Ray Robinson in a fight in London to become world middleweight champion.

July

14th | Judy Garland opens the first of 14 concerts in Dublin, Ireland at the Theatre Royal.

17th | Port Talbot Steelworks opened at Margam, South Wales.

26th | Walt Disney's 13th animated film, Alice in Wonderland, premieres in London, United Kingdom.

31st | Festival Ship Campania is on show in Cardiff Docks as part of the Festival of Britain. Steam tug Earl capsizes while assisting her to berth.

August

15th | Miss World is the oldest running international beauty pageant. It was created in the United Kingdom by Eric Morley in August 1951. Since his death in 2000, Morley's widow, Julia Morley, has co-chaired the pageant. Along with Miss Universe, Miss International and Miss Earth, this pageant is one of the Big Four international beauty pageants—the most coveted beauty titles when it comes to international pageant competitions.

The current Miss World is Vanessa Ponce of Mexico who was crowned on the 8th December 2018 in Sanya, China. She is the first Mexican woman to win Miss World.

The Miss World 2019 Pageant will be held on the 14th December 2019 in London, England.

September

10th | The United Kingdom begins an economic boycott of Iran.

14th | Clement Attlee opens the largest oil refinery in Europe at Fawley on Southampton Water.

23rd | George VI has an operation to remove part of his lung.

26th | Rock and Ice Club formed by a group of climbers in Manchester. The Rock and Ice Club was an English climbing club formed by a group of Manchester climbers. The group regularly climbed on the weekends and met in the week to discuss the past weekend's climbs and plan their future trips.

This loose group crystallized on 26 September 1951 with founding members Nat Allen, Doug Belshaw, Joe Brown, Don Chapman, Don Cowan, Jack Gill, Pete Greenall, Ray Greenall, Ron Moseley, Merrick (Slim) Sorrell, (Instructor Ullswater Outward Bound School) Dick White, Don Whillans.

Notables amongst these founders (in particular Don Whillans and Joe Brown) were at the forefront of British climbing at their time. They were the first British climbers to compete on equal terms with continental alpinists since before the First World War.

30th | Festival of Britain ends.

October

5th With three weeks to go before the second general election in less than two years, opinion polls suggest that the Conservative Party will oust Clement Attlee's Labour government from power after six years, with a majority of 75 to 100 seats and a share of the vote of up to 50%.

6th Malayan Emergency: Communist insurgents kill British commander Sir Henry Gurney.

12th Penrhyn Castle and estate, given to HM Treasury in lieu of death duties, is accepted by the National Trust.

17th The Austin A30 was launched at the 1951 Earls Court Motor Show as the "New Austin Seven" and was Austin's competitor with the Morris Minor. At launch, the car cost £507 (equivalent to £15,793.36 in 2019) undercutting the Minor by £62.

26th The Conservative Party led by Winston Churchill wins the general election, regaining (a month before his seventy-seventh birthday) the position of Prime Minister that he lost six years previously, with a majority of seventeen seats, though with slightly fewer votes than the Labour Party.

28th Sir David Maxwell Fyfe is appointed the first-ever Minister for Welsh Affairs.

30th James Stuart is appointed Secretary of State for Scotland; he will hold office until January 1957.

31st Zebra crossings, a type of pedestrian crossing, introduced for the first time.

Zebra crossings were originally introduced in law by section 18 of the Road Traffic Act 1934. Although the origin of the name is disputed, it is generally attributed to British MP James Callaghan who, in 1948, visited the country's Transport Research Laboratory which was working on a new idea for safe pedestrian crossings. On being shown a black and white design, Callaghan is said to have remarked that it resembled a zebra. After isolated experiments, the zebra crossing was first used at 1,000 sites in the United Kingdom in 1949 in its original form of alternating strips of blue and yellow. They were introduced nationally on the 31st October 1951. In 1971, the Green Cross Code was introduced to teach children safer crossing habits, replacing the earlier "kerb drill".

November

2nd 6,000 British troops are sent to Egypt to deal with anti-British disturbances at Fayid in the Suez Canal Zone.

3rd Express Dairies, owned by 28-year-old Patrick Galvani, open Britain's first full-size supermarket in Streatham Hill, London.

7th The first floodlit Association football match in Scotland, a Stenhousemuir v. Hibernian F.C. friendly at the former's Ochilview Park.

UK bank rate, maintained at 2% since 26 October 1939, is raised.

20th More than 1,000 families of British servicemen begin to move out of the Suez Canal Zone of Egypt after a shooting, which claimed the lives of five British soldiers as well as nine Egyptian civilians.

21st The 1951 Prime Minister's Resignation Honours were officially announced in a supplement to the London Gazette on the 27th November 1951, published on the 30th November 1951, to mark the resignation of the Prime Minister, Clement Attlee.

24th Beinn Eighe in Scotland becomes Britain's first national nature reserve.

29th The Lyons machine was christened Lyons Electronic Office, or LEO. On the recommendation of Wilkes, Lyons recruited John Pinkerton, a radar engineer and research student at Cambridge, as team leader for the project. Lenaerts returned to Lyons to work on the project, and Wilkes provided training for Lyons' engineer Derek Hemy, who would be responsible for writing LEO's programs. On the 15th February 1951 the computer, carrying out a simple test program, was shown to HRH Princess Elizabeth. The first business application to be run on LEO was Bakery Valuations. This was successfully run on the 5th September 1951, and LEO took over Bakery Valuations calculations completely on 29th - 30th November 1951.

December

1st Benjamin Britten's opera Billy Budd is premiered at the Royal Opera House, Covent Garden. When Britten conducted the opera's premiere, in its original form of four acts, it received 17 curtain calls. Uppman was acclaimed as a new star. Billy Budd received its United States première in 1952 in performances by Indiana University Opera Company.

12th John Cockcroft wins the Nobel Prize in Physics jointly with Ernest Walton "for their pioneer work on the transmutation of atomic nuclei by artificially accelerated atomic particles".

25th King George VI makes the Christmas Speech to the Commonwealth, but it has been pre-recorded as he is still struggling to recover from his operation three months ago.

31st Prime Minister Winston Churchill sets off to the United States for talks with President Harry S. Truman.

Save 8 Hours Every Week With A
Hotpoint All-Electric Kitchen

Gain Extra Time For All Your Extra Duties!

YOU'LL DISCOVER wonderful new freedom in a magic Hotpoint All-Electric Kitchen . . . find that it actually saves you over an hour every day, a full working day every single week! You'll feel fresher and have extra time for your family as well as the many added duties you're called on to shoulder these days—because your Hotpoint Kitchen does nearly all of your most tiring, most time-consuming tasks *automatically!*

● ● **Just set the controls** and your Hotpoint Pushbutton Range cooks dinner while you're out shopping! ..Twist a dial and your Hotpoint Electric Dishwasher washes, rinses and dries the dishes! . . . Turn on the water and food waste magically disappears through your Hotpoint Disposall! . . . Special work-saving cabinet arrangements put foods and utensils right at your finger tips! . . .

And you need never waste time defrosting the roomy refrigerator section of your big Hotpoint combination Refrigerator-Freezer!

● ● A Hotpoint All-Electric Kitchen is a real necessity these busy days. And you can easily own one—on convenient monthly terms if you wish. Send today for beautiful new illustrated planning book, "Your Next Kitchen." Mail 15c in coin (no stamps) to Hotpoint, Inc.*, Kitchen & Laundry Planning Dept., 5640 West Taylor Street, Chicago 44, Illinois. *For dealers' names, see your classified phone book.*

Everybody's Pointing To

Hotpoint
Quality Appliances
*A General Electric Affiliate

WORLD'S MOST CONVENIENT REFRIGERATOR!
● ● Out front with everything—that's the new 1951 Hotpoint "Super-Stor" Refrigerator! 72% of all storage space is in finger-tip reach! Your choice of single-door models or 2-door combination Refrigerator-Freezers.

Look To Hotpoint For The Finest . . . *FIRST!*

RANGES • REFRIGERATORS • DISHWASHERS • DISPOSALLS® • WATER HEATERS • FOOD FREEZERS • AUTOMATIC WASHERS • CLOTHES DRYERS • ROTARY IRONERS • CABINETS

Seriously injured! . . .

Oh, she's chirpy enough for the moment . . . *in stockinged feet.* But the harm's been done . . . the harm of big toes bent, of joints enlarged, of bones and muscles hopelessly cramped. And at 15½ that's tragedy.

Avoidable? Of course. Who doesn't know by now that Clarks make absolutely foot-sure shoes — footgauge fitted for length, breadth and girth — in styles to put a gleam into teen-age eyes, in fittings to guard shapeliness in teen-age feet.

Clarks

SHOES FOR TEENAGERS

'CHEYENNE
Unlined calf in tan colour. Sizes 3-8.

PERFECTION IS A MATTER OF TIME

Haig

with the Compliments of the Season

The Oldest Scotch Whisky Distillers in the World · Famous since 1627

"No germs today, thank you!

This is a LIFEGUARD house"

Upstairs and down, inside and out, Lifeguard searches out and destroys the germs. Non-poisonous, non-staining, and so safe to use, you'll enjoy its clean refreshing smell and the confidence it gives. Lifeguard plays a vital part in keeping the family fit. Every home that uses Lifeguard as a regular habit is actively defeating disease germs. There are one-hundred-and-one all-the-year-round uses for Lifeguard.

Safeguard your home the safe way

LIFEGUARD

THE SUPREME DISINFECTANT

Quality

The Guiding Principle in the Manufacture of Ovaltine

CONSIDER the exceptional steps taken in the interests of 'Ovaltine' quality. The 'Ovaltine' Dairy and Egg Farms were established to set the highest standards for the important ingredients used.

The 'Ovaltine' Factory is described as "the ideal of what a food factory should be." Scientific control at every stage of manufacture is maintained by the 'Ovaltine' Research Laboratories, of international repute.

By this insistence on Quality, 'Ovaltine' has achieved outstanding popularity and is an ever-increasing influence for health in every part of the world.

As Quality is all-important where health is concerned, make sure that 'Ovaltine' is your regular daily beverage. Comparatively, it costs so little—it gives so much.

It Pays to Buy the Best

The Ovaltine Factory in a Country Garden

The Ovaltine Dairy Farm with its renowned herd of prize-winning Jersey Cows

The Ovaltine Egg Farm where exceptional conditions assure the production of the highest quality eggs

A. WANDER LTD · BY APPOINTMENT · OVALTINE MANUFACTURERS TO H.M. THE KING

Drink Ovaltine for Health

Delicious HOT or COLD

'Ovaltine' is known on the Continent of Europe as 'Ovomaltine'

P. 750 A

Chocolate — First bite, chocolate... pure Mars milk chocolate, poured on thick as it'll stay!

Almonds — Then crispy, whole almonds, the expensive kind, toasted till they're gold. Plenty of them!

Nougat — Rich, creamy nougat that comes from fresh egg whites and pure sugar, whipped till it's fluffy!

The Candy Bar that's Like a Chocolate Nut Sundae!

The Boys at Mars say:

"We really shot the works to bring you this one!"

How delicious can you get? The answer is—get a Mars Bar and find out. For Mars Bars are made of big choice almonds, fine milk chocolate, pure sugar, top-grade eggs, and good fresh milk right from "down on the farm." These bars are made in the brightest, sunshiniest kitchens you ever saw. Just try one—or two—*you'll* find out.

★MARS BAR 10¢

Toasted Almond

MECCANO MAGAZINE

VOL. XXXVI. No. 6 — JUNE 1951

SOUTHBOUND "ENTERPRISE" LEAVING DUBLIN

9ᴰ

MECCANO MAGAZINE

VOL. XXXVI. No. 5 — MAY 1951

FIGHTERS AFLOAT

9ᴰ

MECCANO MAGAZINE

VOL. XXXVI. No. 11 — NOVEMBER 1951

NEWCASTLE – BRISTOL EXPRESS

9ᴰ

MECCANO MAGAZINE

VOL. XXXVI. No. 12 — DECEMBER 1951

A HAPPY CHRISTMAS

9ᴰ

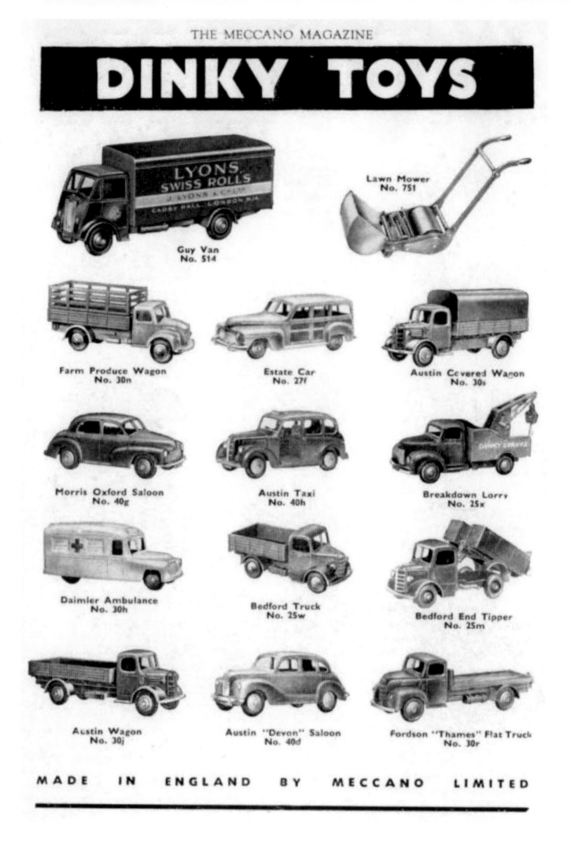

DINKY TOYS

LYONS SWISS ROLLS

Guy Van
No. 514

Lawn Mower
No. 751

Farm Produce Wagon
No. 30n

Estate Car
No. 27f

Austin Covered Wagon
No. 30s

Morris Oxford Saloon
No. 40g

Austin Taxi
No. 40h

Breakdown Lorry
No. 25x

Daimler Ambulance
No. 30h

Bedford Truck
No. 25w

Bedford End Tipper
No. 25m

Austin Wagon
No. 30j

Austin "Devon" Saloon
No. 40d

Fordson "Thames" Flat Truck
No. 30r

MADE IN ENGLAND BY MECCANO LIMITED

Meccano Magazine was an English monthly hobby magazine published by Meccano Ltd between 1916 and 1963, and by other publishers between 1963 and 1981. The magazine was initially created for Meccano builders, but it soon became a general hobby magazine aimed at "boys of all ages". The magazine was launched by Frank Hornby, the inventor of Meccano, as a bi-monthly publication in 1916 in the United States as "Meccano Engineer", and was a month ahead of the UK issue. The first copies were given away free but in 1918 readers had to pay two pence for postage for four issues.

Model 17K7 — Big 17 in. screen...Mahogany or Limed Oak Cabinet.

TV adds so much to family happiness

There's more fun in television than any other family-shared entertainment...comedy, music, sports, drama and educational shows everyone enjoys. Make sure your family gets all this TV fun on the set that brings you *every show at its best*—Motorola TV

PHOTO-PERFECT PICTURES THAT COST YOU LESS

Now—sit close up or far away and enjoy sharp, clear pictures—the product of Motorola's "years ahead" circuit design and advanced engineering features. There's a Motorola to fit your home and pocketbook—from budget-priced table models to luxurious TV-Radio-Phonograph combinations—all with the Motorola Bilt-in-Antenna. Compare—you'll agree —no other offers you so much quality at such low cost.

✓ "GLARE-GUARD" SCREEN

The curved, anti-reflection TV screen that directs annoying reflections *down*—out of your eyes, lets you enjoy your TV more!

✓ FASHION AWARD DESIGN

New beauty for your home, designed with the care given the finest furniture. Styles for modern and traditional settings.

✓ CAMERA VIEW PICTURES

You see all of the picture just as the TV camera "sees" it. The rectangular black tube means brighter, clearer pictures.

✓ "MUSIC LOVER" SOUND

This new sound system brings you true pitch and tone in musical and voice reproduction in full range from bass to treble.

✓ "DEPENDA-BILT" CHASSIS

Factory-tested under extreme conditions to make sure that your Motorola TV will give you the longest, most reliable performance.

✓ TWO SIMPLE CONTROLS

Quick, easy tuning without complicated dialing and adjustments. Just turn it on, then select your station . . . that's all!

you get all these features only in Motorola TV

SEE YOUR CLASSIFIED DIRECTORY FOR YOUR NEAREST MOTOROLA DEALER... *specifications subject to change without notice*

19

The Motor (later, just Motor) was a British weekly car magazine founded on the 28th January 1903 and published by Temple Press. It was initially launched as Motorcycling and Motoring in 1902 before the title was shortened. From the 14th March 1964 issue the magazine name was simply Motor.

In 1988 the journal was absorbed by its long-standing rival Autocar, which became, from the September 7 issue, Autocar & Motor. Six years later, with the 21st September 1994 issue, the name reverted to Autocar.

Famous the World Over

RED TOWER *Pilsner Lager*

BREWED BY RED TOWER LAGER BREWERY LIMITED, MANCHESTER

Sold by leading wine and spirits merchants : served in the best hotels and restaurants

and unequalled in its refreshing qualities for the entertainment of your guests and yourself at home or out-of-doors.

DOLCIS

Fashion Festival 1951

✦ VISITORS TO LONDON ARE INVITED TO SEE ...
IN THE SOUTH BANK EXHIBITION
Shoes chosen for the Festival Design Review.
Shoes specially designed by the Dolcis Studio.
Dolcis craftsmen from our Northamptonshire
factory working in the Power and Production building.

✦ IN THE BATTERSEA PLEASURE GARDENS
A Dolcis shoe shop — the only shoe shop in the Exhibition.

✦ IN THE TRAVELLING EXHIBITION FASHION SHOWS
Dolcis fashion shoes worn by the Mannequins.

✦ IN 16 WEST END DOLCIS SHOPS
within easy reach of South Bank

✦ IN 200 DOLCIS SHOE STORES THROUGHOUT GREAT BRITAIN
specially designed FESTIVAL STROLLERS and SANDALS
and a wonderful collection of fashion shoes.

distinctively **DOLCIS**
the name for fashion shoes

Enquiries should be addressed to
Dolcis Festival Enquiry Bureau, Dolcis House, 7-13 Great Dover Street, London, S.E.1. Telephone: HOP 3551

. . . for 1951 — and for the years to come

The 'Prestige' housewares you buy in 1951 will still
be making light work of kitchen tasks long after the
Festival of Britain has become a memory. The
'Prestige' range comprises pressure cookers,
hollow-ground cutlery and kitchen tools in styles
to suit every taste, at prices to suit all purses.

Prestige

Three favourite items are illustrated: the
'Prestige' Commodore Pressure Cooker (top);
'Prestige' Hollow-ground Cutlery (centre);
and the 'Prestige' 1900 series Kitchen
Tools (bottom). But *every* item
'made by the 'Prestige' people' is
soundly made, brilliantly styled and
superbly finished, to give the utmost value
and the greatest efficiency. Ask for 'Prestige'
Housewares at your local stores or ironmongers.

PLATERS & STAMPERS LIMITED — *Prestige House, 14/18 Holborn, London, E.C.1*

Somebody has to be first !

You have only to taste it to know why "Black & White"
keeps growing in popularity. Blended in the special
"Black & White" way it is a Scotch that is a
joy to drink at all times and for all occasions.

"BLACK & WHITE"
SCOTCH WHISKY

The Secret is in the Blending

By Appointment
to H.M. King George VI
Scotch Whisky Distillers
James Buchanan & Co. Ltd.

Maximum Prices (U.K. only) as fixed by the Scotch Whisky Association

---

**From
SUNRISE to SUNSET**

*Everyday
is an*

OXO

DAY

for the beefy, family drink

Compare it with any washer, at any price...see how

Only *Thor* gives you all 4

1 Hydro-Swirl washing action!

Thor's Hydro-Swirl principle of washing lets the water do the work. It swishes and swirls clothes gently but thoroughly, washes them cleaner, faster, yet safely. And proved best by test in laboratory *and home!*

2 Saves 27 gallons hot water!

The 1951 Thor beats the 8 other leading automatic or semi-automatic washers in economy! Saves up to 27 gallons of hot water every washday for a family of 4! Proved by test! And Thor saves soap, saves fuel costs, too.

3 Controllable washing time!

No fixed mechanical cycles! You decide how much water—how long to wash each load. Then flick the switch. Thor washes, rinses, spins clothes damp dry—in one single tub! Your hands never touch hot, soapy water!

4 Thor-way overflow rinse!

Look! Dirt and suds float up and off the top, *not down through the clothes,* as in ordinary washers. And the 1951 Thor has finger-tip control . . . lets you rinse (as well as wash) for as long or short a period as you like.

No Other Washer Gives You All These Washday Advantages!

Count the blessings of this marvelous 1951 Thor Spinner Washer! 1.Hydro-Swirl Washing Action! 2.Super Saving of Hot Water! 3.Controllable Washing Time! 4.The Thor-Way Overflow Rinse! What a combination! What a washer!

Today, look in the classified phone directory for the name of your nearest Thor dealer. Ask for a demonstration of the 1951 Thor Spinner Washer with Hydro-Swirl Washing Action!

And be sure to see the Thor Dryer (Electric or Gas), Thor Wringer Washer, Thor Gladiron, Thor Combination Sink. For more efficient homemaking . . . depend on Thor, leaders in home laundry appliances for over 45 years! *Thor Corporation, Chicago 50, Ill.*

Thor *so Spinner-washer with Hydro-Swirl Action*

No Plumbing Installation Necessary! • No Bolting Down! • No Annoying Vibration!

COST OF LIVING 1951

A conversion of pre-decimal to decimal money

The Pound, 1971 became the year of decimalization when the pound became 100 new pennies. Prior to that the pound was equivalent to 20 shillings. Money prior to 1971 was written £/s/d. (d being for pence). Below is a chart explaining the monetary value of each coin before and after 1971.

Symbol	Before 1971	After 1971
£	**Pound (240 pennies)**	**Pound (100 new pennies)**
s	Shilling (12 pennies)	5 pence
d	**Penny**	**¼ of a penny**
¼d	Farthing	1 penny
½d	**Halfpenny**	**½ pence**
3d	Threepence	About 1/80 of a pound
4d	**Groat (four pennies)**	
6d	Sixpence (Tanner)	2½ new pence
2s	**Florin (2 shillings)**	**10 pence**
2s/6d	Half a crown (2 shillings and 6 pence)	12½ pence
5s	**Crown**	**25 pence**
10s	10 shilling note (10 bob)	50 pence
10s/6d	**½ Guinea**	**52½ pence**
21s	1 Guinea	105 pence

Prices are in equivalent to new pence today and on average throughout the UK.

Item	1951	Price equivalent today
Wages, average yearly	**£334.00**	**£10,640.00**
Average house price	£1,994.00	£61,615.00
Price of an average car	**£615.00**	**£19,004.00**
Litre of petrol	£0.04p	£1.13p
Flour 1.5kg	**£0.06p**	**£1.70p**
Bread (loaf)	£0.03p	£0.77p
Sugar 1kg	**£0.06p**	**£1.70p**
Milk 1 pint	£0.09p	£2.84p
Butter 250g	**£0.07p**	**£2.13p**
Cheese 400g	£0.05p	£1.59p
Potatoes 2.5kg	**£0.04p**	**£1.31p**
Bacon 400g	£0.18p	£5.44p
Beer (Pint)	**£0.05p**	**£1.59p**

In the 1950s, the average cost of a house was just under £2000 and the average worker took home around £10 a week. So buying a house was no mean feat even then.

If you could afford to buy a house in the 1950s, it was likely to be a new one. Half a million homes had been destroyed by German bombing, so when the war came to an end, houses had to be built, and fast. The result was pre-fab houses and brand new estates on the outskirts of our cities.

The first pre-fabs went up in June 1945, just a few weeks after the war had ended. Built in just 40 man-hours (often by prisoners of war), they came with hot water, heating and newly fitted kitchens and bathrooms. They became fondly known as the "people's palaces" and, although they were meant as a temporary solution, some are still standing today.

The new houses of the 1950s must have seemed like the height of luxury compared to the bombed terraces and slum conditions many families had been living in.

This was the time when Brits everywhere were introduced to the joys of going to the toilet inside – and having proper toilet paper when they got there!

The 1950s also introduced us to life-changing inventions such as the electric fire, washing machine and every mother's favourite - the fish finger.

BRITISH BIRTHS

Philip David Charles Collins LVO was born on the 30th January 1951and is an English drummer, singer, songwriter, multi-instrumentalist, record producer, and actor. He was the drummer and later became singer of the rock band Genesis, and is also a solo artist. Born and raised in Chiswick, West London, Phil Collins played drums from the age of five and completed drama school training, which secured him various roles as a child actor. He then pursued a music career, joining Genesis in 1970 as their drummer and becoming lead singer in 1975 following the departure of Peter Gabriel. Phil began a solo career in the 1980s, initially inspired by his marital breakdown and love of soul music, releasing a series of successful albums, including Face Value (1981), No Jacket Required (1985), and ...But Seriously (1989). In 1996, Collins left Genesis to focus on solo work; this included writing songs for Disney's Tarzan (1999) for which he received an Oscar for Best Original Song for "You'll Be in My Heart". He re-joined Genesis for their Turn It On Again Tour in 2007.

Joseph Kevin Keegan, OBE was born on the 14th February 1951 and is an English former football player and manager. Kevin grew up in Armthorpe, Doncaster, England. As a player in the 1970s and 1980s, he has been described as "arguably the first superstar English player to attract the modern media spotlight". He began his playing career at Scunthorpe United in 1968, before moving to Liverpool in 1971. At Liverpool, Kevin Keegan won three First Division titles, the UEFA Cup twice, the FA Cup and the European Cup. He also gained his first England cap in 1972, and moved to West German club Hamburger SV in the summer of 1977. At Hamburg, he was named European Footballer of the Year in 1978 and 1979, won the Bundesliga title in 1978–79. He moved into management at Newcastle in 1992, winning promotion as First Division champions. Newcastle then finished second in the Premier League in 1995–96, after leading for most of the season. He took charge of the England team in February 1999, but resigned in October 2000, following a 1–0 loss against Germany.

Jane Seymour, OBE was born Joyce Penelope Wilhelmina Frankenberg on the 15th February 1951 and is an British-American actress. Jane grew up in Uxbridge, London, England. In 1969, Jane Seymour appeared uncredited in her first film, Richard Attenborough's Oh! What a Lovely War. In 1973, Seymour achieved international fame in her role as Bond girl Solitaire in the James Bond film Live and Let Die. IGN ranked her as 10th in a Top 10 Bond Babes list. In 1980, Seymour played the role on stage of Constanze in Peter Shaffer's play Amadeus, opposite Ian McKellen as Salieri and Tim Curry as Mozart. The play premiered on Broadway in 1980, ran for 1,181 performances and was nominated for seven Tony Awards, of which it won five. In 1988, Seymour got the female lead in the 12-part television miniseries War and Remembrance. In the 1990s, Jane Seymour earned popular and critical praise for her role as Dr. Michaela "Mike" Quinn in the television series Dr. Quinn, Medicine Woman and its television sequels (1993–2001). Her work on the series earned her a second Golden Globe Award.

James Gordon Brown HonFRSE was born on the 20th February 1951and is a British politician who was prime minister of the United Kingdom and leader of the Labour Party from 2007 to 2010. Gordon Brown grew up in the town of Giffnock, Renfrewshire, Scotland. A doctoral graduate of the University of Edinburgh, Gordon Brown spent his early career working as both a lecturer at a further education college and a television journalist. He entered Parliament in 1983 as the MP for Dunfermline East. He joined the shadow cabinet in 1989 as shadow secretary of State for Trade, and was later promoted to become shadow chancellor of the Exchequer in 1992. After Labour's victory in 1997, he was appointed chancellor of the Exchequer, becoming the longest-serving holder of that office in modern history. Tony Blair resigned as Prime Minister and Labour Leader in 2007, and Gordon Brown was chosen to replace him in an uncontested election. On the 10th May 2010, Brown announced he would stand down as leader of the Labour Party.

Sir Kenneth Mathieson Dalglish MBE was born on the 4th March 1951 and is a Scottish former football player and manager. Kenny Dalglish began his career with Celtic in 1971, going on to win four Scottish league championships, four Scottish Cups and one Scottish League Cup with the club. In 1977, Liverpool manager Bob Paisley paid a British transfer record of £440,000 to bring Dalglish to Liverpool. His years at Liverpool were among the club's most successful periods, as he won six English league championships, the FA Cup, four League Cups, five FA Charity Shields, three European Cups and one European Super Cup. Kenny Dalglish became player-manager of Liverpool in 1985 after the resignation of Joe Fagan, winning a further three First Divisions, an FA Cup and four FA Charity Shields, before resigning in 1991. Eight months later, Dalglish made a return to football management with Blackburn Rovers, whom he led from the Second Division to win the Premier League in 1995. Kenny Dalglish returned to Anfield as a non-executive director, and had Anfield's Centenary Stand renamed after him in May 2017.

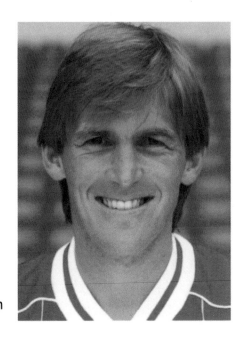

Christopher Anton Rea was born on the 4th March 1951 and is an English rock and blues singer-songwriter and guitarist. Born and raised in Middlesbrough, he is of Italian and Irish descent. In the United States he is best known for the 1978 song "Fool (If You Think It's Over)", which reached No. 12 on the Billboard Hot 100 and spent three weeks at No. 1 on the Adult Contemporary chart. This success earned him a Grammy nomination as Best New Artist in 1979. In 1973 he joined the local Middlesbrough band, Magdalene, which earlier had included David Coverdale who had left to join Deep Purple. He began writing songs for the band and only took up singing because the singer in the band failed to show up for a playing engagement. Rea then went on to form the band The Beautiful Losers which received Melody Maker's Best Newcomers award in 1973. His 10th studio album was Rea's major breakthrough. The Road to Hell (1989) enjoyed massive success and became his first No. 1 album in the UK, being certified 6× Platinum by the BPI in 2004. Rhino released on the 18th October 2019 a 2CD deluxe editions of five of Chris Rea's most commercially successful albums.

Peter Davison born Peter Malcolm Gordon Moffett on the 13th April 1951and is an English actor with many credits in television dramas and sitcoms. He chose the stage name Peter Davison to avoid confusion with the actor and director Peter Moffatt. His first television work was a 1975 episode of the children's science fiction television programme The Tomorrow People, alongside American actress Sandra Dickinson, whom he married on the 26th December 1978. In 1978, Peter Davison's performance as the youthfully mischievous Tristan Farnon in All Creatures Great and Small made him a household name. In 1980, Davison signed a contract to play the Doctor for three years, succeeding Tom Baker (the Fourth Doctor) and, at age 29, was at the time the youngest actor to have played the lead role. In 2017 Davison appeared in an episode of the third series of Grantchester, playing a cricket-loving solicitor. Davison appeared with Christopher Timothy in the three-part series Vintage Roads Great & Small in 2018.

Julian Lloyd Webber was born on the 14th April 1951 and is a British solo cellist. Lloyd Webber made his professional debut at the Queen Elizabeth Hall, London, in September 1972 when he gave the first London performance of the cello concerto by Sir Arthur Bliss. Demonstrating his involvement in music education, he formed the Music Education Consortium with James Galway and Evelyn Glennie in 2003. As a result of successful lobbying by the Consortium, on the 21st November 2007, the UK government announced an infusion of £332 million for music education. Lloyd Webber has represented the music education sector on programmes such as BBC1's Question Time, The Andrew Marr Show, BBC2's Newsnight and BBC Radio 4's Today. On the 28th April 2014, Lloyd Webber announced his retirement from public performance as a cellist because of a herniated disc in his neck. His final public performance as a cellist was on the 2nd May 2014 at the Festival Theatre, Malvern, with the English Chamber Orchestra when he played the Barjansky Stradivarius cello which he had played for more than thirty years.

Louise Jameson was born on the 20th April 1951 and is an English actress. Louise Jameson was born in Wanstead, London. She attended the Royal Academy of Dramatic Art and spent two years with the Royal Shakespeare Company, performing in Romeo and Juliet, The Taming of the Shrew, King Lear, Summerfolk, and Blithe Spirit. Her early TV career highlights included appearances on Emmerdale in 1973 (as Sharon Crossthwaite), as Leela, the leather-clad barbarian warrior companion of the fourth Doctor in Doctor Who (1977–78). In 1998, Jameson began a long run in the BBC soap EastEnders as Rosa di Marco, appearing in over 200 episodes over two and a half years until August 2000. Later, she has appeared in episodes of the BBC Scotland soap River City as Viv Roberts, as a guest artist in episodes of Doctors, Holby City and The Bill, and as a regular in Doc Martin. In 2013, Louise starred in the play Gutted by Rikki Beadle-Blair and has been nominated for Best Female Performance at the 2013 Off West End Theatre Awards. In 2016, she toured in Agatha Christie's The Mousetrap, the longest running show in British theatre.

John Anthony Conteh, MBE was born on the 27th May 1951 and is a British former professional boxer. He was born and raised in Toxteth, Liverpool, Lancashire, England. He competed from 1971 to 1980. He held the WBC light-heavyweight title from 1974 to 1978, and regionally the European, British and Commonwealth titles between 1973 and 1974. John Conteh began boxing at the age of 10 at a boxing club in Kirkby that was a training ground for some of the best amateur boxers, such as Joey Singleton, Tucker Hetherington and Stuart Morton. At 19, he won the middleweight gold medal at the 1970 British Commonwealth Games. Outside if boxing Conteh was one of the celebrities featured dressed in prison gear on the cover of the 1973 Wings album, Band on the Run. Conteh also appeared in films such as Man at the Top (1973), The Stud (1978) and Tank Malling (1989), and made a starring appearance in the television show Boon in 1989.
John Conteh was appointed Member of the Order of the British Empire (MBE) in the 2017 Birthday Honours for services to boxing.

Bonnie Tyler born Gaynor Hopkins on the 8th June 1951 is a Welsh singer, known for her distinctive husky voice. She grew up in a small town called Skewen, in Neath, Wales. Bonnie Tyler came to prominence with the release of her 1977 album The World Starts Tonight and its singles "Lost in France" and "More Than a Lover". Her 1978 single "It's a Heartache" reached number four on the UK Singles Chart, and number three on the US Billboard Hot 100. In the 1980s, Tyler ventured into rock music with songwriter and producer Jim Steinman. He wrote Tyler's biggest hit "Total Eclipse of the Heart", the lead single from her 1983 UK chart topping album Faster Than the Speed of Night. Steinman also wrote Tyler's other major 1980s hit "Holding Out for a Hero". Rocks and Honey was released in 2013 and features the single "Believe in Me" which she performed representing the United Kingdom at the Eurovision Song Contest 2013 in Malmö, Sweden. Her latest album Between the Earth and the Stars was released on the 15th March 2019.

John Richard Deacon was born on the 19th August 1951 and is an English retired musician, best known for being the bass guitarist for the rock band Queen. John Deacon grew up in Oadby, Leicestershire, playing bass in a local band, The Opposition, before moving to study electronics at Chelsea College, London. He joined Queen in 1971 on the strength of his musical and electronic skills, particularly the home-made Deacy Amp which guitarist Brian May used to create guitar orchestras throughout Queen's career. From the third album, Sheer Heart Attack, onwards, he wrote at least one song per album, several of which became hits. As well as bass, Deacon played some guitar and keyboards on Queen's studio work. He composed several songs for the group—including Top 10 hits "You're My Best Friend", "Another One Bites the Dust", "Back Chat", and "I Want to Break Free"—and was involved in the band's financial management. After the death of lead singer Freddie Mercury in 1991 and the following year's Tribute Concert, Deacon performed only sporadically with the remaining members of Queen before retiring from the music industry in 1997 after recording "No-One but You (Only the Good Die Young)".

David Coverdale was born on the 22nd September 1951 and is an English rock singer best known for his work with Whitesnake, a hard rock band he founded in 1978. David grew up in a seaside town called Saltburn-by-the-Sea in North Riding of Yorkshire, England. In 1973 David Coverdale saw an article in a copy of Melody Maker, which said that Deep Purple was auditioning for singers to replace Ian Gillan. David had fronted a local group called The Government, which had played with Deep Purple on the same bill in 1969, so he and the band were familiar with one another, and after sending a tape and later auditioning, Coverdale was admitted into the band. After the demise of Deep Purple, Coverdale embarked on a solo career. He released his first album in February 1977, titled White Snake. After recording Northwinds, Coverdale soon formed the band Whitesnake, with Bernie Marsden and Micky Moody both handling guitar duties. In 2000 Coverdale released his first solo album in 22 years, titled Into The Light. Even though the album was not a hit, it did return Coverdale to the music business.

Gordon Matthew Thomas Sumner CBE was born on the 2nd October 1951 and known as Sting. He is an English musician and actor. Sting grew up in a town called Wallsend, Northumberland, England. He was the principal songwriter, lead singer, and bassist for the new wave rock band the Police from 1977 to 1984, and launched a solo career in 1985. As a solo musician and a member of the Police, Sting has received 17 Grammy Awards: he won Song of the Year for "Every Breath You Take", three Brit Awards, including Best British Male Artist in 1994 and Outstanding Contribution in 2002, a Golden Globe, an Emmy and four nominations for the Academy Award for Best Original Song. In 2019, he received a BMI Award for "Every Breath You Take" becoming the most played song in radio history. With the Police, Sting became one of the world's best-selling music artists. Solo and with the Police combined, he has sold over 100 million records. Sting's fourteenth album, titled My Songs, was released on the 24th May 2019. The album features 14 studio re-recorded versions of his songs released throughout his solo career and his time with the Police.

William McGuire Bryson OBE HonFRS was born on the 8th December 1951 and is an American-British author of books on travel, the English language, science, and other non-fiction topics. Born in the United States, he has been a resident of Britain for most of his adult life, returning to the United States between 1995 and 2003, and holds dual American and British citizenship. He served as the chancellor of Durham University from 2005 to 2011. Bill Bryson first visited Britain in 1973 during his tour of Europe and decided to stay after landing a job working in a psychiatric hospital. While living in the US in the 1990s Bryson wrote a column for a British newspaper for several years, reflecting on humorous aspects of his repatriation in the United States. These columns were selected and adapted to become his book I'm a Stranger Here Myself. In 2005 Bryson was appointed chancellor of Durham University, succeeding the late Sir Peter Ustinov. He was awarded an honorary Officer of the Order of the British Empire (OBE) for his contribution to literature on the 13th December 2006. In 2011 he won the Golden Eagle Award from the Outdoor Writers and Photographers Guild.

BRITISH DEATHS

Edith Bessie New was born on the 17th March 1877 and passed away on the 2nd January 1951 and was an English suffragette. She was one of the first two suffragettes to use vandalism as a tactic. She and Mary Leigh were surprised to find their destruction was celebrated and they were pulled triumphantly by lines of suffragettes on their release in 1908. In the early 1900s New left her teaching career and began working as an organiser and campaigner for the Women's Social and Political Union (WSPU). She travelled around England speaking to groups about the women's movement. In January 1908, Edith New and Olivia Smith chained themselves to the railings of 10 Downing Street shouting "Votes for Women!" to create a diversion for their fellow suffragettes Flora Drummond and Mary Macarthur to sneak in before being arrested. Later in June 1908 during a protest, New and another suffragette, Mary Leigh, broke two windows at 10 Downing Street. They were arrested and sentenced to two months in prison at Holloway. Edith New retired to the holiday community of Polperro in Cornwall and died in early 1951, aged 73.

Sir Percy Malcolm Stewart, 1st Baronet was born on the 9th May 1872 and died on the 27th February 1951. He was an English industrialist and philanthropist. He incorporated The London Brick Company in the 1920s which was at the time reputed to be the largest brick making company in the United Kingdom.

The cement business in which the family was interested - B. J. Forder & Son Ltd - became part of the British Portland Cement Manufacturers Ltd in 1912, and Stewart became a managing director. He had remained managing director of the brick division of B. J. Forder & Son until it was amalgamated into The London Brick Company in 1923, and Stewart became chairman of its board. He became chairman of the board of the Associated Portland Cement Manufacturers Ltd. (APCM) in 1924 and remained in that position until 1945 when he became company president. He was thus chairman of the two of the largest monopolistic companies in British industry.

Ivor Novello was born on the 15th January 1893 and died on the 6th March 1951. He was born David Ivor Davies, and was a Welsh composer and actor who became one of the most popular British entertainers of the first half of the 20th century. He was born into a musical family, and his first successes were as a songwriter. His first big hit was "Keep the Home Fires Burning" (1914), which was enormously popular during the First World War. His 1917 show, Theodore & Co, was a wartime hit. In the 1920s, he turned to acting, first in British films and then on stage, with considerable success in both. He starred in two silent films directed by Alfred Hitchcock, The Lodger and Downhill (both 1927). On stage, he played the title character in the first London production of Liliom (1926). Novello died suddenly from a coronary thrombosis at the age of 58, a few hours after completing a performance in the run of King's Rhapsody. He was cremated at the Golders Green Crematorium, and his ashes are buried beneath a lilac bush and marked with a plaque that reads "Ivor Novello 6th March 1951 'Till you are home once more'."

Ernest Bevin was born on the 9th March 1881 and passed away on the 14th April 1951. He was a British statesman, trade union leader, and Labour politician. He co-founded and served as general secretary of the powerful Transport and General Workers' Union in the years 1922–1940, and as Minister of Labour in the war-time coalition government. He succeeded in maximising the British labour supply, for both the armed services and domestic industrial production, with a minimum of strikes and disruption.

His most important role came as Foreign Secretary in the post-war Labour government, 1945–1951. He gained American financial support, strongly opposed Communism, and aided in the creation of NATO. Bevin's tenure also saw the end of the Mandate of Palestine and the creation of the State of Israel. His biographer, Alan Bullock, said that Bevin "stands as the last of the line of foreign secretaries in the tradition created by Castlereagh, Canning and Palmerston in the first half of the 19th century".

Joseph Paton Maclay, 1st Baron Maclay PC was born on the 6th September 1857 and died on the 24th April 1951. He was known as Sir Joseph Maclay, 1st Baronet, from 1914 to 1922 and was a Scottish businessman and public servant. Joseph Maclay was created a baronet, of Park Terrace in the City of Glasgow in the County of Lanark, in 1914 and in 1922 he was raised to the peerage as Baron Maclay, of Glasgow in the County of Lanark. Maclay opposed nationalisation of merchant shipping and insisted that owners still be allowed to make a profit as an incentive, although excessive profits were taxed. Maclay approved four standard designs of merchant ship and began the process of increasing ship construction, although he was hampered by shortages of steel and labour, and ships under construction in the USA were confiscated when she entered the war. Maclay rejected Admiral Jellicoe's arguments that convoys presented too large a target to U-boats, and that merchant ship masters lacked the discipline to "keep station" in a convoy (from personal experience, he knew the latter to be false).

Robert Broom FRS FRSE was born on the 30th November 1866 and died on the 6th April 1951. He was a Scottish South African doctor and palaeontologist. He qualified as a medical practitioner in 1895 and received his DSc in 1905 from the University of Glasgow. Broom was first known for his study of mammal-like reptiles. After Raymond Dart's discovery of the Taung Child, an infant australopithecine, Broom's interest in palaeoanthropology was heightened. Broom's career seemed over and he was sinking into poverty, when Dart wrote to Jan Smuts about the situation. Smuts, exerting pressure on the South African government, managed to obtain a position for Broom in 1934 with the staff of the Transvaal Museum in Pretoria as an Assistant in Palaeontology. The remainder of Broom's career was devoted to the exploration of these sites and the interpretation of the many early hominin remains discovered there. He continued to write to the very last. Shortly before his death he finished a monograph on the Australopithecines and remarked to his nephew: "Now that's finished ... and so am I."

SPORTING EVENTS 1951

1951 County Cricket Season

1951 was the 52nd season of County Championship cricket in England. It produced a surprise title for Warwickshire, their first for forty years and only the second in their history. It was noteworthy for the period in being the first achieved under a professional captain, Tom Dollery, one of the Wisden Cricketers of the Year in 1952. His award particularly noted his captaincy. It was a comfortable victory as Warwickshire won 16 matches while second-placed Yorkshire won four less and lost twice convincingly to Warwickshire.

Warwickshire County Cricket Club is one of eighteen first-class county clubs within the domestic cricket structure of England and Wales. It represents the historic county of Warwickshire. Its 50 overs team is called the Warwickshire Bears and its T20 team the Birmingham Bears. Founded in 1882, the club held minor status until it was elevated to first-class in 1894 pending its entry into the County Championship in 1895. Since then, Warwickshire have played in every top-level domestic cricket competition in England. The club's home is Edgbaston Cricket Ground in south Birmingham, which regularly hosts Test and One-Day International matches.

Team	Pld	W	L	LWF	DWF	DTF	DLF	ND	Pts
Warwickshire (C)	28	16	2	0	6	0	4	0	216
Yorkshire	28	12	3	0	10	0	1	2	184
Lancashire	28	8	1	1	9	0	5	4	136
Worcestershire	28	9	5	2	4	0	6	2	132
Glamorgan	28	8	3	1	7	0	6	3	128
Surrey	28	7	6	0	9	0	4	2	120
Middlesex	28	7	5	1	7	0	6	2	116
Essex	28	6	2	0	9	1	8	2	110
Hampshire	28	5	6	1	9	0	4	3	100
Sussex	28	6	6	0	5	1	9	1	94
Derbyshire	28	5	4	2	6	0	10	1	92
Gloucestershire	28	5	8	1	6	0	6	2	88
Northamptonshire	28	4	3	1	7	0	10	3	80
Somerset	28	5	12	3	1	0	5	2	76
Leicestershire	28	4	7	0	4	0	12	1	64
Kent	28	4	14	1	2	0	6	1	60
Nottinghamshire	28	1	11	0	7	0	6	3	40

1950–51 in English football

Tottenham Hotspur won their first League Championship, while Newcastle United defeated Blackpool 2–0 to win their fourth FA Cup. They would win it twice more over the next four seasons. Everton were relegated to the Second Division for only the second time in their history.

The league was expanded from 88 to 92 clubs for this season, with Scunthorpe United and Shrewsbury Town joining the Third Division North and Colchester United join the Third Division South along with Gillingham who were re-elected to the league 12 years after being voted out of it.

Sunderland signed Trevor Ford from Aston Villa for the then record fee of £30,000 (2012: £900,000).

At the end of the season, Matt Busby signed Birmingham City winger Johnny Berry for Manchester United for a club record fee of £25,000.

Pos	Team	Pld	W	D	L	GF	GA	GR	Pts
1	Tottenham Hotspur	42	25	10	7	82	44	1.864	60
2	Manchester United	42	24	8	10	74	40	1.850	56
3	Blackpool	42	20	10	12	79	53	1.491	50
4	Newcastle United	42	18	13	11	62	53	1.170	49
5	Arsenal	42	19	9	14	73	56	1.304	47
6	Middlesbrough	42	18	11	13	76	65	1.169	47
7	Portsmouth	42	16	15	11	71	68	1.044	47
8	Bolton Wanderers	42	19	7	16	64	61	1.049	45
9	Liverpool	42	16	11	15	53	59	0.898	43
10	Burnley	42	14	14	14	48	43	1.116	42
11	Derby County	42	16	8	18	81	75	1.080	40
12	Sunderland	42	12	16	14	63	73	0.863	40
13	Stoke City	42	13	14	15	50	59	0.847	40
14	Wolverhampton Wanderers	42	15	8	19	74	61	1.213	38
15	Aston Villa	42	12	13	17	66	68	0.971	37
16	West Bromwich Albion	42	13	11	18	53	61	0.869	37
17	Charlton Athletic	42	14	9	19	63	80	0.788	37
18	Fulham	42	13	11	18	52	68	0.765	37
19	Huddersfield Town	42	15	6	21	64	92	0.696	36
20	Chelsea	42	12	8	22	53	65	0.815	32
21	Sheffield Wednesday	42	12	8	22	64	83	0.771	32
22	Everton	42	12	8	22	48	86	0.558	32

1950–51 Scottish Division One

The 1950–51 Scottish Division One was won by Hibernian by ten points over nearest rival Rangers. Clyde and Falkirk finished 15th and 16th respectively and were relegated to the 1951–52 Scottish Division Two.

Pos	Team	Pld	W	D	L	GF	GA	GD	Pts
1	Hibernian	30	22	4	4	78	26	+52	48
2	Rangers	30	17	4	9	64	37	+27	38
3	Dundee	30	15	8	7	47	30	+17	38
4	Heart of Midlothian	30	16	5	9	72	45	+27	37
5	Aberdeen	30	15	5	10	61	50	+11	35
6	Partick Thistle	30	13	7	10	57	48	+9	33
7	Celtic	30	12	5	13	48	46	+2	29
8	Raith Rovers	30	13	2	15	52	52	0	28
9	Motherwell	30	11	6	13	58	65	−7	28
10	East Fife	30	10	8	12	48	66	−18	28
11	St Mirren	30	9	7	14	35	51	−16	25
12	Morton	30	10	4	16	47	59	−12	24
13	Third Lanark	30	11	2	17	40	51	−11	24
14	Airdrieonians	30	10	4	16	52	67	−15	24
15	Clyde	30	8	7	15	37	57	−20	23
16	Falkirk	30	7	4	19	35	81	−46	18

1950–51 Scottish Division Two

The 1950–51 Scottish Second Division was won by Queen of the South who, along with second placed Stirling Albion, was promoted to the First Division. Alloa Athletic finished bottom.

Pos	Team	Pld	W	D	L	GF	GA	GD	Pts
1	Queen of the South	30	21	3	6	69	35	+34	45
2	Stirling Albion	30	21	3	6	78	44	+34	45
3	Ayr United	30	15	6	9	64	40	+24	36
4	Dundee United	30	16	4	10	78	58	+20	36
5	St Johnstone	30	14	5	11	68	53	+15	33
6	Queen's Park	30	13	7	10	56	53	+3	33
7	Hamilton Academical	30	12	8	10	65	49	+16	32
8	Albion Rovers	30	14	4	12	56	51	+5	32
9	Dumbarton	30	12	5	13	52	53	−1	29
10	Dunfermline Athletic	30	12	4	14	58	73	−15	28
11	Cowdenbeath	30	12	3	15	61	57	+4	27
12	Kilmarnock	30	8	8	14	44	49	−5	24
13	Arbroath	30	8	5	17	46	78	−32	21
14	Forfar Athletic	30	9	3	18	43	76	−33	21
15	Stenhousemuir	30	9	2	19	51	80	−29	20
16	Alloa Athletic	30	7	4	19	58	98	−40	18

1951 Five Nations Championship

The 1951 Five Nations Championship was the twenty-second series of the rugby union Five Nations Championship. Including the previous incarnations as the Home Nations and Five Nations, this was the fifty-seventh series of the northern hemisphere rugby union championship. Ten matches were played between the 13th January and the 7th April. It was contested by England, France, Ireland, Scotland and Wales. Ireland missed out on a second Grand Slam after drawing to Wales at Cardiff Arms Park despite winning the title.

Table

Position	Nation	Games				Points			Table points
		Played	Won	Drawn	Lost	For	Against	Difference	
1	Ireland	4	3	1	0	21	16	+5	7
2	France	4	3	0	1	41	27	+14	6
3	Wales	4	1	1	2	29	35	−6	3
4	Scotland	4	1	0	3	39	25	+14	2
4	England	4	1	0	3	13	40	−27	2

Results

France	14–12	Scotland
Wales	23–5	England
Ireland	9–8	France
Scotland	19–0	Wales
Ireland	3–0	England
England	3–11	France
Scotland	5–6	Ireland
Wales	3–3	Ireland
England	5–3	Scotland
France	8–3	Wales

Nation	Venue	City	Captain
England	Twickenham	London	Vic Roberts/John Kendall-Carpenter
France	Stade Olympique Yves-du-Manoir	Colombes	Guy Basquet
Ireland	Lansdowne Road	Dublin	Karl Mullen
Scotland	Murrayfield	Edinburgh	Peter Kininmonth
Wales	National Stadium/St. Helens	Cardiff/Swansea	John Gwilliam/Jack Matthews

The Masters 1951

The 1951 Masters Tournament was the 15th Masters Tournament, held April 5–8 at Augusta National Golf Club in Augusta, Georgia. Ben Hogan, age 38, won the first of his two Masters titles, two strokes ahead of runner-up Skee Riegel. It was the fifth of his nine major titles.

After three rounds, Hogan was one stroke out of the lead, behind Riegel and Sam Snead, the 1949 champion. Hogan shot a bogey-free final round of 68 (−4), while Riegel carded a 71 and Snead an 80 (+8). Prior to this victory, Hogan had eight top ten finishes at the Masters, twice as runner-up in 1942 and 1946.

The reigning U.S. Open champion, Hogan also won the year's next major, the 1951 U.S. Open.

With high attendance of about 15,000 on Sunday, a fifty percent bonus for the prize money was declared, boosting the purse to $15,000 and the winner's share to $3,000.

Place	Player	Country	Score	To par	Money ($)
1	**Ben Hogan**	🇺🇸 United States	70-72-70-68=280	−8	3,000
2	Skee Riegel	🇺🇸 United States	73-68-70-71=282	−6	1,875
T3	Lloyd Mangrum	🇺🇸 United States	69-74-70-73=286	−2	1162
T3	Lew Worsham	🇺🇸 United States	71-71-72-72=286	−2	1162
5	Dave Douglas	🇺🇸 United States	74-69-72-73=288	E	750
6	Lawson Little	🇺🇸 United States	72-73-72-72=289	+1	600
7	Jim Ferrier	🇦🇺 Australia	74-70-74-72=290	+2	525
T8	Johnny Bulla	🇺🇸 United States	71-72-73-75=291	+3	450
T8	Byron Nelson	🇺🇸 United States	71-73-73-74=291	+3	450
T8	Sam Snead	🇺🇸 United States	69-74-68-80=291	+3	450

Augusta National Golf Club, sometimes referred to as Augusta or the National, is one of the most famous and exclusive golf clubs in the world, located in Augusta, Georgia, United States. Unlike most private clubs which operate as non-profits, Augusta National is a for-profit corporation, and it does not disclose its income, holdings, membership list, or ticket sales.

Founded by Bobby Jones and Clifford Roberts, the course was designed by Jones and Alister Mackenzie and opened for play in 1932. Since 1934, the club has played host to the annual Masters Tournament, one of the four major championships in professional golf, and the only major played each year at the same course. It was the top-ranked course in Golf Digest's 2009 list of America's 100 greatest courses and was the number ten-ranked course based on course architecture on Golf week Magazine's 2011 list of best classic courses in the United States.

Cheltenham Gold Cup 1951

Silver Fame was a British Thoroughbred racehorse who won the 1951 Cheltenham Gold Cup. After beginning his racing career in Ireland he moved to England and became one of the leading steeplechasers of his time. He won races at the Cheltenham Festival in 1948 and 1950 and ran twice in the Grand National, falling when favourite for the race in 1948. Despite running extremely well at Cheltenham he did not contest the Gold Cup until 1951 when he won the race in record time. He was also the oldest winner of the race up to that time, and remains one of only two horses to win the race at the age of twelve. He spent his retirement as a hunter.

Until 1951 Silver Fame had never contested the Cheltenham Gold Cup. For last two renewals Lord Bicester had preferred to rely on Finnure who had finished fourth in 1949 and second in 1950.

Triple Crown

2,000 Guineas

Ki Ming was an Irish-bred British-trained Thoroughbred racehorse and sire best known for winning the classic 2000 Guineas in 1951. As a two-year-old he showed promise to win at Royal Ascot but his season was disrupted when his trainer was banned for a doping offence. At three, he recorded an upset win over a large field to win the Guineas but failed when favourite for The Derby. In autumn he returned to sprint distances and won the Diadem Stakes at Ascot. His record as a breeding stallion was very disappointing.

St Leger

Talma was a French Thoroughbred racehorse and sire best known for winning the classic St Leger Stakes. After winning his first two races in France he started second favourite for the St Leger and won by a margin conservatively recorded as ten lengths despite misbehaving before the race. He recorded his only other win of any consequence when he took the Cumberland Lodge Stakes. He raced until the age of five and was then exported to South America where he had moderate success as a breeding stallion.

The Derby

Arctic Prince was an Irish-bred Thoroughbred racehorse and sire who was trained in England during a brief racing career which lasted from 1950 to 1951 and consisted of only five races. Arctic Prince won two races including the 1951 Epsom Derby and was retired after breaking down at Ascot in July of the same year.

As a three-year-old, Arctic Prince was sent directly to the 2000 Guineas at Newmarket Racecourse without a trial race. He ran on strongly in the closing stages of the one mile Classic to finish seventh of the twenty-seven runners behind Ki Ming.

1951 British Grand Prix

The 1951 British Grand Prix was a Formula One motor race held on the 14th July 1951 at the Silverstone Circuit in Northamptonshire, England. It was race 5 of 8 in the 1951 World Championship of Drivers and was contested over 90 laps. The race was the first victory for José Froilán González, and was also the first of many for the Scuderia Ferrari team. Both the team and driver also achieved their first ever pole position during the weekend.

Final Placings

Pos	No	Driver	Constructor	Laps	Time/retired	Grid	Points
1	12	José Froilán González	Ferrari	90	2:42:18.2	1	8
2	2	Juan Manuel Fangio	Alfa Romeo	90	+51.0	2	6
3	10	Luigi Villoresi	Ferrari	88	+2 laps	5	4
4	4	Felice Bonetto	Alfa Romeo	87	+3 laps	7	3
5	6	Reg Parnell	BRM	85	+5 laps	20	2
6	3	Consalvo Sanesi	Alfa Romeo	84	+6 laps	6	
7	7	Peter Walker	BRM	84	+6 laps	19	
8	9	Brian Shawe-Taylor	ERA	84	+6 laps	12	
9	14	Peter Whitehead	Ferrari	83	+7 laps	8	
10	22	Louis Rosier	Talbot-Lago-Talbot	83	+7 laps	9	

1951 Wimbledon Championships

The 1951 Wimbledon Championships took place on the outdoor grass courts at the All England Lawn Tennis and Croquet Club in Wimbledon, London, United Kingdom. The tournament was held from Monday 25th June until Saturday 7th July 1951. It was the 65th staging of the Wimbledon Championships, and the third Grand Slam tennis event of 1951.

Men's Singles

In the 1951 Wimbledon Championships – Gentlemen's Singles tennis competition, Dick Savitt defeated Ken McGregor in the final, 6–4, 6–4, 6–4 to win the title. He was the second ever American to win the Wimbledon and Australian tournaments in the same year. Number 4 seed Budge Patty was the defending champion, but lost in the second round to another American, the unseeded 17-year-old Ham Richardson.

Women's Singles

Doris Hart defeated Shirley Fry in the final, 6–1, 6–0 to win the Ladies' Singles tennis title at the 1951 Wimbledon Championships. Louise Brough was the defending champion, but lost in the semi-finals to Fry.

Men's Doubles

Ken McGregor and Frank Sedgman defeated Jaroslav Drobný and Eric Sturgess in the final, 3–6, 6–2, 6–3, 3–6, 6–3 to win the Gentlemen' Doubles tennis title at the 1951 Wimbledon Championship.

Women's Doubles

Shirley Fry and Doris Hart defeated the defending champions Louise Brough and Margaret duPont in the final, 6–3, 13–11 to win the Ladies' Doubles tennis title at the 1951 Wimbledon Championships.

Mixed Doubles

Frank Sedgman and Doris Hart defeated Rose and Bolton in the final, 7–5, 6–3 to win the Mixed Doubles tennis title at the 1951 Wimbledon Championships.

Doris Hart was the star of Wimbledon in 1951 winning the singles, doubles and mixed doubles.

Doris Hart was a tennis player from the United States who was active in the 1940s and first half of the 1950s. She was ranked World No. 1 in 1951. She was the fourth player, and second woman, to win a Career Grand Slam in singles. She was the first of only three players (all women) to complete the career "Boxed Set" of Grand Slam titles, which is winning at least one title in singles, women's doubles, and mixed doubles at all four Grand Slam events. Only Margaret Smith Court and she achieved this during the amateur era of the sport. Court claimed an additional Boxed Set in the open era and the only other player to claim one is Martina Navratilova.

BOOKS PUBLISHED IN 1951

They Came To Baghdad. A secret summit of superpowers is to be held in Baghdad, but it is no longer secret. A shadowy group (which is both anti-Communist and anti-Capitalist) is plotting to sabotage the event. Things get complicated when enthusiastic young "adventurer" Victoria Jones discovers a dying secret British agent – Henry "Fakir" Carmichael – in her hotel room. His last words – "Lucifer...Basrah...Lefarge" – propel her into investigation. "Lucifer" refers to the mastermind, Victoria's false lover Edward, who is behind the plot. "Basrah" is the city where Carmichael saw Edward and recognised him as an enemy. "Lefarge" turns out to actually be "Defarge" and is a reference to a Charles Dickens character; it is an allusion to the fact that the name of a vital witness has been stitched into a scarf. While Victoria is the central character, the real heroine is Anna Scheele, secretary/executive assistant to an American banker, who has discovered a great deal about finances of the shadowy group. She appears rather sparingly, with a few brief appearances in the early part of the story, then seems to vanish, to the chagrin of the evil organization who fear her financial knowledge and who want to liquidate her, and of her allies who wish to protect her. She is presumed dead by her allies but she reappears at the eleventh hour in a most surprising manner.

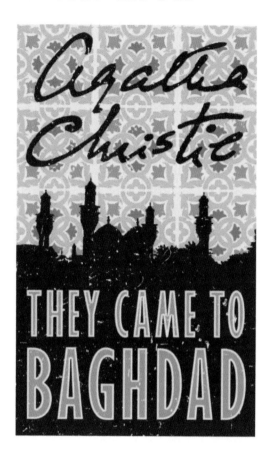

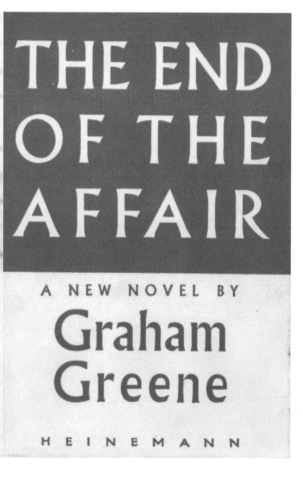

The End Of The Affair. The novel focuses on Maurice Bendrix, a rising writer during the Second World War in London, and Sarah Miles, the wife of an impotent civil servant. Bendrix is based on Greene himself, and he reflects often on the act of writing a novel. Sarah is based on Greene's lover at the time, Catherine Walston, to whom the book is dedicated. Bendrix and Sarah fall in love quickly, but he soon realises that the affair will end as quickly as it began. The relationship suffers from his overt and admitted jealousy. He is frustrated by her refusal to divorce Henry, her amiable but boring husband. When a bomb blasts Bendrix's flat as he is with Sarah, he is nearly killed. After this, Sarah breaks off the affair with no apparent explanation. Later, Bendrix is still wracked with jealousy when he sees Henry crossing the Common that separates their flats. Henry has finally started to suspect something, and Bendrix decides to go to a private detective to discover Sarah's new lover. Through her diary, he learns that, when she thought he was dead after the bombing, she made a promise to God not to see Bendrix again if He allowed him to live again. Greene describes Sarah's struggles. After her sudden death from a lung infection brought to a climax by walking on the Common in the rain, several miraculous events occur, advocating for some kind of meaningfulness to Sarah's faith.

Prince Caspian (originally published as Prince Caspian: The Return to Narnia) is a high fantasy novel for children by C. S. Lewis, published by Geoffrey Bles in 1951. It was the second published of seven novels in The Chronicles of Narnia (1950–1956), and Lewis had finished writing it in 1949, before the first book was out. It is volume four in recent editions of the series, sequenced according to the internal chronology of the books. Like the others, it was illustrated by Pauline Baynes and her work has been retained in many later editions.

Prince Caspian features a "return to Narnia" by the four Pevensie children of the first novel, about a year later in England but 1300 years later in Narnia. It is the only book of The Chronicles with men dominating Narnia. The talking animals and mythical beings are oppressed, and some may be endangered. The English siblings, legendary Kings and Queens of Narnia, are magically recalled, once again children, by the refugee Prince Caspian.

Macmillan US published an American edition within the calendar year.

Prince Caspian has been adapted and filmed as two episodes of BBC television series in 1989 and as a feature film in 2008.

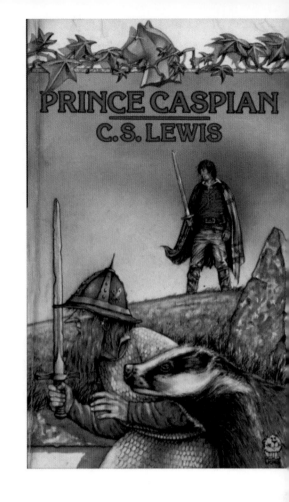

The Cruel Sea is a 1951 novel by Nicholas Monsarrat. It follows the lives of a group of Royal Navy sailors fighting the Battle of the Atlantic during the Second World War. It contains seven chapters, each describing a year during the war.

The novel, based on the author's experience of serving in corvettes and frigates in the North Atlantic in the Second World War, gives a matter-of-fact but moving portrayal of ordinary men learning to fight and survive in a violent, exhausting battle against the elements and a ruthless enemy.

The action commences in 1939. Lieutenant-Commander George Ericson, a Merchant Navy and Royal Naval Reserve officer, is recalled to the Royal Navy and given command of the fictitious Flower-class corvette HMS Compass Rose, newly built to escort convoys. The crew cross the Atlantic many times on escort duty in all kinds of weather, often encountering fierce storms in one of the smallest ships built to protect Allied convoys. The men endure the ship's constant rolling and pitching in the huge waves, freezing cold, the strain of maintaining station on the convoy on pitch-black nights and the fear that at any second a torpedo from a German U-boat could blow them to oblivion.

A Question of Upbringing is the opening novel in Anthony Powell's A Dance to the Music of Time, a twelve-volume cycle spanning much of the 20th century.

Published in 1951, it begins the story of a trio of boys, Nicholas Jenkins (the narrator), Charles Stringham, and Peter Templer, who are friends at a nameless school (based upon Powell's public school Eton College) and then move on to different paths.

A fourth figure, Kenneth Widmerpool, stands slightly apart from them, poised for greatness.

The title of the book had its origin in an incident in which Powell was a passenger in a car driven by his friend, the Old Etonian screenwriter, Thomas Wilton ("Tommy") Phipps.

Phipps and Powell found themselves driving straight towards an oncoming vehicle. Powell later recorded, "Seizing the hand-brake as we sped towards what seemed imminent collision, Phipps muttered to himself, 'This is just going to be a question of upbringing.'"

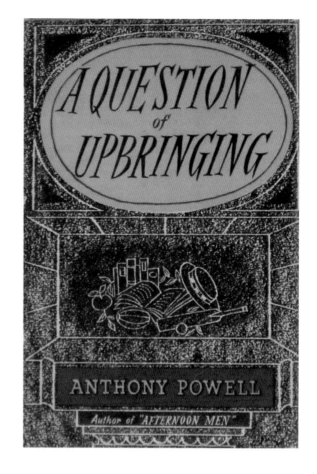

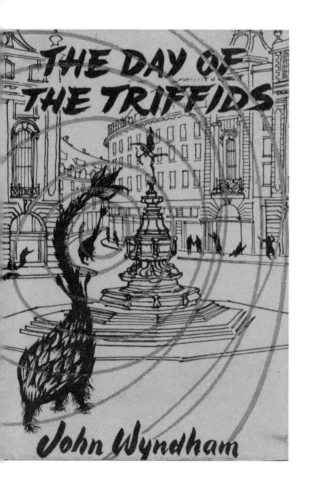

The Day of the Triffids is a 1951 post-apocalyptic novel by the English science fiction author John Wyndham. After most people in the world are blinded by an apparent meteor shower, an aggressive species of plant starts killing people. Although Wyndham had already published other novels using other pen name combinations drawn from his real name, this was the first novel published as "John Wyndham".

The story has been made into the 1962 feature film of the same name, three radio drama series (in 1957, 1968 and 2001) and two TV series (in 1981 and 2009). It was nominated for the International Fantasy Award in 1952 and in 2003 the novel was listed on the BBC's survey The Big Read. It was the inspiration for the zombie movie 28 Days Later.

During The Blitz, Wyndham was a firewatcher and later member of the Home Guard. He witnessed the destruction of London from the rooftops of Bloomsbury. He described many scenes and incidents, including the uncanny silence of London on a Sunday morning after a heavy bombardment, in letters to his long-term partner Grace Wilson. These found their way into The Day of the Triffids.

A Christmas Carol. Ebenezer Scrooge (Alastair Sim) is a greedy businessman who thinks only of making money. For him, Christmas is, in his own words, a humbug. It has been seven years since his friend and partner, Jacob Marley (Sir Michael Hordern), died and on Christmas Eve. Marley's ghost tells him he is to be visited during the night by three spirits. The Ghost of Christmas Past (Michael Dolan) revisits some of the main events in Scrooge's life to date, including his unhappy childhood, his happy apprenticeship to Mr. Fezziwig (Roddy Hughes), who cared for his employees, and the end of his engagement to a pretty young woman due to a growing love of money. The Ghost of Christmas Present (Francis De Wolff) shows him how joyously is nephew Fred (Brian Worth) and his clerk, Bob Cratchit (Mervyn Johns), celebrate Christmas with those they love. The Ghost of Christmas Yet to Come (Czeslaw Konarski) shows him what he will leave behind after he is gone. Scrooge awakens on Christmas morning, a new man intent on doing well and celebrating the season with all of those around him.

Run time is 1h 26mins

Trivia

Sir Michael Hordern was not on-set when the "Marley's Ghost" segment was filmed. He was added in later through the use of an optical printer. He only appeared together with Alastair Sim in the two scenes at the end of the "Ghost of Christmas Past" sequence, the latter of the two being the scene where Jacob Marley dies. This was also true of Michael Dolan (Spirit of Christmas Past). He never actually played any scenes on the set with Sim.

Although the word "Scrooge" means a stingy person now, in Charles Dickens' time, the word was a slang term meaning "to squeeze".

The opening credits clearly show that "Scrooge" is the original name of this British movie, an "adaptation of Charles Dickens' 'A Christmas Carol'." The name of this movie was changed for its American release to match the name of Dickens' book.

Goofs

In an early scene, Scrooge refuses Samuel Wilkins' request for a Christmas postponement, by saying "You'd still owe me £20 you're not in a position to repay if it was the middle of a heatwave on an August Bank Holiday". This refers to a law enacted in 1871, after Charles Dickens' death.

When Scrooge and Marley offer to buy up the company from Mr. Jorkin, the medium shots show Marley with his hands in his vest pockets, but every close-up has his hands clasped on his stomach.

A Streetcar Named Desire. Set in the French Quarter of New Orleans during the restless years following World War Two, A STREETCAR NAMED DESIRE is the story of Blanche DuBois, a fragile and neurotic woman on a desperate prowl for someplace in the world to call her own. After being exiled from her hometown of Laurel, Mississippi, for seducing a seventeen-year-old boy at the school where she taught English, Blanche explains her unexpected appearance on Stanley and Stella's (Blanche's sister) doorstep as nervous exhaustion. This, she claims, is the result of a series of financial calamities which have recently claimed the family plantation, Belle Reve. Suspicious, Stanley points out that "under Louisiana's Napoleonic code what belongs to the wife belongs to the husband." Stanley, a sinewy and brutish man, is as territorial as a panther. He tells Blanche he doesn't like to be swindled and demands to see the bill of sale. This encounter defines Stanley and Blanche's relationship. They are opposing camps and Stella is caught in no-man's-land. But Stanley and Stella are deeply in love. Blanche's efforts to impose herself between them only enrage the animal inside Stanley. When Mitch -- a card-playing buddy of Stanley's -- arrives on the scene, Blanche begins to see a way out of her predicament.

Run time 2h 02mins

Trivia

Fitted t-shirts could not be bought at the time, so Marlon Brando's apparel had to be washed several times and then the back stitched up, to appear tightly over the actor's chest.

Vivien Leigh had already played Blanche in the first London production of the play, under the direction of her then-husband, Laurence Olivier. She later said that Olivier's direction of that production influenced her performance in the film more than Elia Kazan's direction of the film did.

The Production Code censors demanded 68 script changes from the Broadway staging, while the interference of the Catholic Legion of Decency led to even further cuts, most of them having to do with references to homosexuality and rape. In his memoirs, Tennessee Williams wrote that he liked the film but felt it was "slightly marred by the Hollywood ending."

Goofs

When Stanley comes back from taking Stella to the hospital, he is looking for a bottle opener. He finds it on the mantelpiece, shakes up a bottle of beer, and opens it. The beer foams up and spills on his trousers. But if you watch at the moment when he swings himself up to sit on the table - before he opens the bottle - you can see that the fronts of his trousers are already wet. Apparently they re-shot it without him changing into dry trousers.

Just after Stanley goes through Blanche's things, his shirt goes from fairly dry, to two distinct spots on his chest, to soak all the way down the front, in a matter of seconds.

Stanley says he served in the 241st Engineers and fought in the Battle of Salerno. However the 241st Engineer Combat Battalion fought in the Asiatic-Pacific Area, not in Europe.

Alice in Wonderland. Extremely late for a very important meeting, the befuddled, White Rabbit, stumbles upon little Alice, in this Walt Disney's loose adaptation of Lewis Carroll's namesake fantasy extravaganza. Without much thought, down the rabbit hole Alice goes, deep into Wonderland's colourful realm, where she can grow bigger--or smaller--and funny creatures such as the Mad Hatter, the Caterpillar, the March Hare, and the Cheshire Cat congregate around large tables at noisy tea parties. Of course, a kingdom is not complete without a king and his queen--the tyrannical, Queen of Hearts--who has a thing for heads. Will Alice stay forever in this magical dream-world?

Box Office
Budget:$3,000,000 (estimated)

Oscar Nominee: Best Music, Scoring of a Musical Picture

Run time 1h 15mins.

Trivia

In the Walrus and the Carpenter sequence, the R in the word "March" on the mother oyster's calendar flashes. This alludes to the old adage about only eating oysters in a month with an R in its name. That is because those months without an R (May, June, July, August) are the summer months in England, when oysters would not keep due to the heat, in the days before refrigeration.

This movie is actually a combination of Lewis Carroll's two "Alice" books, "Alice's Adventures in Wonderland" and "Through the Looking Glass".

The movie took five years to complete, but was in development for over ten years before it entered active production.

Goofs

During "The Walrus and the Carpenter", the appearance of the walrus' eyes is inconsistent between shots. Some shots have just little black dot eyes, while some shots have him with full pupils and coloured eyes.

During the tea party, the "half a cup" changes its configuration, and the seating arrangement changes when the March Hare is smacked with a hammer. Although probably not intentional, these goofs fit in with the absurd, disorienting humour of the scene.

Towards the end of the scene with the flowers, the flowers are asking Alice what kind of flower she is. There's a shot from above, looking down on Alice. Behind her, we see her shadow on the ground. Although Alice is moving a bit, the shadow is perfectly still.

The African Queen. September 1914, news reaches the colony German Eastern Africa that Germany is at war, so Reverend Samuel Sayer became a hostile foreigner. German imperial troops burn down his mission; he is beaten and dies of fever. His well-educated, snobbish sister Rose Sayer buries him and leaves by the only available transport, the dilapidated river steamboat 'African Queen' of grumpy Charlie Allnut. As if a long difficult journey without any comfort weren't bad enough for such odd companions, she is determined to find a way to do their bit for the British war effort (and avenge her brother) and aims high, as God is obviously on their side: construct their own equipment, a torpedo and the converted steamboat, to take out a huge German warship, the Louisa, which is hard to find on the giant lake and first of all to reach, in fact as daunting an expedition as anyone attempted since the late adventurous explorer John Speakes, but she presses till Charlie accepts to steam up the Ulana, about to brave a German fort, raging rapids, very bloodthirsty parasites and the endlessly branching stream which seems to go nowhere but impenetrable swamps.

Run time 1h 40mins

Trivia

Sources claimed that everyone in the cast and crew got sick except Humphrey Bogart and John Huston, who said they avoided illness by essentially living on imported Scotch whiskey. Bogart later said, "All I ate was baked beans, canned asparagus and Scotch whiskey. Whenever a fly bit Huston or me, it dropped dead."

The African Queen was actually the L.S. Livingston, which had been a working diesel boat for 40 years; the steam engine was a prop and the real diesel engine was hidden under stacked crates of gin and other cargo. It is now docked next to the Holiday Inn in Key Largo, FL, just off US Highway 1.

Humphrey Bogart won the Academy Award for Best Actor for his performance in this movie, making him the last man born in the 19th century to ever win a leading role Oscar.

Goofs

Charlie refers to the boat as 30 foot long. It is clearly nowhere near that length, in actuality being only 16 foot.

On first evening on African Queen, while Rose is drinking her tea, the shadow of the boom mic appears over the port edge of the boat several times.

In some close-ups of the African Queen, her name is painted in white letters. Other shots show the name of the boat in black lettering.

When Charlie climbs back onto the boat after diving under the water to inspect the damage to the propeller and shaft, his hair and upper torso are clearly dry.

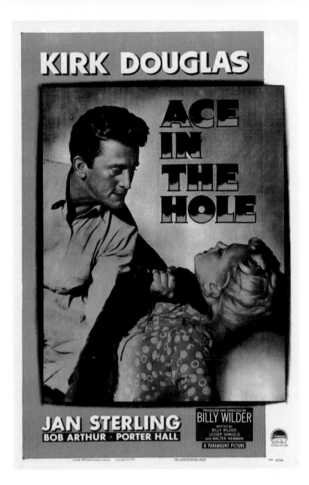

Ace in the Hole. The cynical, unethical and unscrupulous journalist Chuck Tatum arrives at a small New Mexico newspaper asking for a chance. He was fired from famous newspapers because of drinking, lying and even for having an affair with the wife of one of his bosses. His real intention is to use the small newspaper as a platform to reach a bigger one. After one year without any sensational news and totally bored, Chuck travels with a younger reporter to cover a story about rattlesnakes. When they arrive at an isolated gas station, he is informed that a man called Leo Minosa is trapped alive in an old Indian mine in a nearby place called the Mountain of the Seven Vultures. Chuck manipulates the local corrupt sheriff, the engineer responsible for the rescue operation and Leo's wife Lorraine Minosa, so that a rescue that could have been made in twelve hours lasts six days using a sophisticated drilling system. Chuck Tatum uses the time to create a media circus. Everybody profits from the accident - everybody except the victim.

Box Office
Budget:$1,800,000 (estimated)

Run time 1h 51mins

Trivia
In a 1950 memo to Billy Wilder, Kirk Douglas objected to several aspects of Chuck Tatum's monologue about missing New York City: "No pastrami! No garlic pickles! No Madison Square Garden! No Yogi Berra!", among other things. Douglas asked, "... what the hell is a Yogi Berra?" Douglas' secretary, who was amused her boss didn't know who the New York Yankee star was, told him he was a catcher.

Residents of Gallup, New Mexico, were hired as extras. They were paid 75 cents an hour for a ten-hour day. Extras earned an additional three dollars if they could bring an automobile to the set.

Kirk Douglas was borrowed by Paramount from Warner Bros. and was paid a fee of $150,000 for his portrayal.

Goofs
When entering Mr. Boot's office at the beginning of the movie: The folder and newspaper in his left hand change position between cameras from outside and inside the office.

When Lorraine and Chuck are talking out in front of Minosa's store by the gas pumps, reflections of the crew moving around behind the camera can be seen in the store windows.

When Tatum and Herbie walk out to their dust-covered car after all the people left, handprints from where Tatum leans on the car can be seen in the dust indicating that they shot the scene numerous times and decided to put one of the later takes in the movie.

The Day the Earth Stood Still. Travelling with mind-boggling speed, a gleaming unidentified flying object zooming in from the boundless deep space, penetrates the Earth's atmosphere, landing smoothly in Cold War-Washington, D.C. Encircled by large yet feeble military forces, the peaceful intergalactic ambassador, Klaatu, emerges from the mysterious vessel accompanied by the silently dangerous robot of incomprehensible power, Gort, only to witness first-hand the earthlings' hospitality.

The sophisticated humanoid declares that he comes in peace; however, he needs to assemble the world's greatest minds to hear his merciful warning and a definitive ultimatum. Is Klaatu the messenger of humanity's doom?

Box Office
Budget: $1,200,000 (estimated)

Golden Globe Winner:
Best Film Promoting International Understanding

Run time 1h 32mins

Trivia

Lock Martin, the doorman at Grauman's Chinese Theatre, was cast because of his nearly seven-foot height. However, he was not a physically strong man and could not actually carry Patricia Neal, and so had to be aided by wires (in shots from the back where he's carrying her, it's actually a lightweight dummy in his arms). He also had difficulty with the heavy Gort suit and could only stay in it for about a half hour at a time.

As an homage to this film, George Lucas named three of Jabba the Hutt's alien henchman in his Star Wars Return of the Jedi, "Klaatu", "Baroda" and " Niko".

The Army refused to cooperate after reading the script. The studio then approached the National Guard, which had no qualms about seeing the Army depicted in a less-than-flattering light, and gladly offered their cooperation.

Goofs

After Klaatu is shot from behind, the soldiers who examine him make no attempt to apprehend Helen, despite the fact that she was just speaking to Klaatu in full view of them, and obviously knows him.

The British radar man says it's moving at 4,000 mph. Then says it must be a Buzz bomb. As a British radar man, he'd know that the Buzz bomb only flew at 360 mph 75% were shot down by the English air force.

When Klaatu visits Dr. Barnhardt in the evening, there is a small piece of paper pinned to one side of the blackboard, the left side. On the paper is seen (briefly) "Do Not Erase". A few moments later in the same scene, there is no paper pinned to the side of the blackboard. Again, in the same scene, the paper is back very briefly, but just as before, disappeared almost immediately.

Showboat. The "Cotton Blossom", owned by the Hawk family, is the show boat where everyone comes for great musical entertainment down south. Julie LaVerne and her husband are the stars of the show. After a snitch on board calls the local police that Julie (who's half- African-American) is married to a white man, they are forced to leave the show boat. The reason being, that down south interracial marriages are forbidden.

Magnolia Hawk, Captain Andy Hawks' daughter, becomes the new show boat attraction and her leading man is Gaylord Ravenal, a gambler. The two instantly fall in love, and marry, without Parthy Hawks's approval. Magnolia and Gaylord leave the "Cotton Blossom" for a whirl-wind honeymoon and to live in a Pl: fantasy world. Magnolia soon faces reality quickly, that gambling means more to Gaylord than anything else. Magnolia confronts Gaylord and after he gambles away their fortune he leaves her - not knowing she is pregnant. Magnolia is left penniless and pregnant, and is left to fend for herself, and make a new start.

Run time 1h 48mins

Trivia

Director George Sidney was forced to leave for a few days because of illness, so uncredited associate producer Roger Edens directed the beautifully shot, fog-enshrouded "departure" sequence, including the performance by William Warfield of "Ol' Man River." It is the one scene in the film that has been praised even by critics who detest this version of "Show Boat."

The original choice for the role of Julie was Judy Garland, but since she had ended her contract with MGM, the idea of casting Garland was dropped. Dinah Shore was next in line until the role finally went to Ava Gardner. It is myth that Lena Horne was ever seriously considered for Julie, as she was no longer under contract to MGM and, by 1951, was not a big enough box office draw.

It reportedly took only one take for William Warfield to pre-record his rendition of "Ol' Man River" prior to filming.

Goofs

In the opening scenes with the calliope player, the keyboard is a contemporary 1950's black console, whereas a period console would have been made of wood, and perhaps elaborately carved and detailed.

When the townspeople are rushing to see the show boat at the beginning, the camera crew's shadow is visible on the road.

When the Cotton Blossom is pulling away from the dock, at the end of the movie, you can see big clouds of blue smoke pouring out the right side of the ship (near the rear). These are definitely exhaust gases from either a gas or diesel engine that is installed in the ship, and most likely used to power the paddle wheel.

Captain Horatio Hornblower. In 1807, Captain Horatio Hornblower leads his ship the HMS Lydia on a perilous voyage around Cape Horn and into the Pacific. The men, even his officers, don't know exactly where he is leading them. England is at war with Napoleon and everyone wonders why they have been sent so far from the action. They eventually arrive on the Pacific coast of Central America where the HMS Lydia has been sent to arm Don Julian Alvarado, who is planning an attack against France's Spanish allies on the North American continent. The hope is that Alvarado's forces will require the French to divert some of their military resources to North American defence in the aid of their Spanish allies. He arrives to learn that a Spanish Galleon is en route and he no sooner captures it and hands it over to Alvarado that he learns the Spanish are now England's allies and he must take it from Alvarado. He also gets a very comely passenger in the form of Lady Barbara Wellesley, sister of the Duke of Wellington. The voyage is uneventful but Horatio and Barbara develop a deep affection for one another, despite that he is married and she is engaged. There are more battles ahead however for Hornblower and he finds himself under the command of Admiral Leighton, Barbara's new husband.

Run time 1h 34mins

Trivia

The ship Lieutenant William Bush (Robert Beatty) and Captain Horatio Hornblower (Gregory Peck) board to meet the Admiral at the end of the movie is the actual H.M.S. Victory, currently dry-docked at Portsmouth, England. As Admiral Horatio Nelson's flagship at Trafalgar, she is still commissioned to the present day as an official vessel of the Royal Navy, and the only surviving original ship of the line still in existence.

The rights to the novel were originally acquired by Warner Brothers with Errol Flynn in mind, but after the financial failure of The New Adventures of Don Juan (1948), and growing difficulties with the actor, he was not cast. Warner Brothers was already building up Burt Lancaster as its new swashbuckler, but the role of a British Sea Captain seemed out of his range, so Gregory Peck was ultimately cast.

Goofs

Hornblower asks whether Lady Barbara is related to the Duke of Wellington. This is in 1807. Sir Arthur Wellesley was elevated to the Peerage after the Battle of Talavera and to a Dukedom in 1814 after the Army invaded France. In 1807 he was still Sir Arthur. The title of Duke of Wellington did not exist.

At one point Hornblower and his officers give the loyal toast whilst seated. While it is true that the Royal Navy do toast the King or Queen seated, this tradition only dates to the reign of William IV (1830-1837), aka the Sailor King. At the date when this film is set, RN officers would still have got to their feet to toast the King.

Set in 1807, the Lieutenants on Hornblower's ship all display the single shoulder epaulet - a rank insignia for Lieutenants which was not adopted by the Royal Navy until after 1812.

Detective Story. In the 21st Precinct of New York, criminals are booked after being arrested: a shoplifter is brought after stealing a purse in a department store; two burglars with extensive criminal record are captured by a policeman; the small time embezzler Arthur Kindred, who is primary and without any resistance. The tough Detective McLeod is an honest detective with strong principles and code of honour, who loves his wife Mary. He is near to conclude a case against an abortionist, Dr. Karl Schneider, with the testimony of a witness that is coming to identify Dr. Schneider. However, the woman is bribed and the upset McLeod hits Schneider, and he insinuates to McLeod's chief, Lt. Monaghan that the problem is personal and gives the name of Mary McLeod. Lt. Monaghan invites Mary to come to the precinct for investigation, when deep inner secrets are disclosed leading to a tragedy.

Academy Awards Nominee Oscar:
Best Actress in a Leading Role: Eleanor Parker
Best Actress in a Supporting Role: Lee Grant
Best Director: William Wyler
Best Writing, Screenplay: Philip Yordan, Robert Wyler

Run time 1h 43mins

Trivia

The USS Juneau, mentioned by Detective Brody, was a light cruiser sunk at the Battle of Guadalcanal in November 1942. Its loss was notable for the deaths of five brothers from the one family, the Sullivan's.

William Wyler engaged Dashiell Hammett to adapt the Sidney Kingsley play for the screen. After three weeks Hammett returned the advance check to Wyler, saying he couldn't do it. At the time Hammett was under scrutiny for his alleged Communist affiliations and was blacklisted.

The role of Detective McLeod was originally offered to Alan Ladd.

The play ran on Broadway for 581 performances, from 23 March 1949-12 August 1950. It starred Ralph Bellamy as Det. McLeod. Meg Mundy played his wife. Maureen Stapleton played Miss Hatch, and James Westerfield was Lou Brody.

At 20 minutes and 10 seconds, Eleanor Parker's performance in this movie is the shortest to ever be nominated for a Best Actress Oscar.

Goofs

In some of the close-up shots of McLeod and Schneider in the back of the paddy wagon, McLeod's shadow can be faintly seen on the rear-projection screen showing the street behind them. (Other shadows can also be seen.)

About 40 minutes into the film, Jim McLeod misidentifies himself as "Dan McLeod of W.85 St".

Pandora and the Flying Dutchman. Albert Lewin's interpretation of the legend of the Flying Dutchman. In a little Spanish seaport named Esperanza, during the 30s, appears Hendrick van der Zee, the mysterious captain of a yacht (he is the only one aboard). Pandora is a beautiful woman (who men kill and die for). She's never really fallen in love with any man, but she feels very attracted to Hendrick...

We are soon taught that Hendrick is the Flying Dutchman, this sailor of the 17th century that has been cursed by God to wander over the seas until the Doomsday... unless a woman is ready to die for him...

Box Office

Budget:$1,500,000 (estimated)
Cumulative Worldwide Gross: $14,404

Run time 2h 02mins

Trivia

The great Welsh poet Dylan Thomas showed up for the location shoot of the race car speed test on the beach at Pendine Sands, which was near his home in Wales. He can be spotted briefly at the start of the scene, at 1:11:03-04, as the hat less man in the brown jacket and beige trousers at the extreme left of the crowd in the background (ignoring the family of three on the left) about one-fourth of the picture's width from the left. This is the only known surviving motion picture footage of Thomas.

Photographed in the English Technicolor process by Jack Cardiff, this film is considered one of the most beautiful colour films ever made.

Ava Gardner says in her biography that the actor Marion Cabre, who plays the bullfighter in love with her in the movie, wanted to do the same in real life. According to her, he was a real pain in the ass.

The famous poet Dylan Thomas visited the set and is believed to have appeared as an extra, being briefly visible in the background in one scene.

Goofs

Most of the story takes place in 1930, but the costumes and hairstyles of Ava Gardner, as well as those of Sheila Sim and Pamela Mason are strictly in the 1950s mode.

When Hendrik begins reading the diary the desk lamp is on his right, but when Geoffrey turns it on, it is on Hendrik's left. No one has moved it in the meantime.

In the workroom where Stephen is repairing his race car, the words "NON FUMAR" are written on the wall, with the English words "NO SMOKING" beneath. The Spanish is incorrect: it should read "NO FUMAR".

The Lavender Hill Mob. Holland, a shy retiring man, dreams of being rich and living the good life. Faithfully, for twenty years, he has worked as a bank transfer agent for the delivery of gold bullion. One day he befriends Pendlebury, a maker of souvenirs. Holland remarks that, with Pendlebury's smelting equipment, one could forge the gold into harmless-looking toy Eiffel Towers and smuggle the gold from England into France.

Soon afterwards, the two plant a story to gain the services of professional criminals Lackery and Shorty. Together, the four plot their crime, leading to unexpected twists and turns.

Oscar Winner: **Best Writing, Story and Screenplay**
T.E.B. Clarke
Oscar Nominee: **Best Actor in a Leading Role**
Alec Guinness

BAFTA Winner: Best British Film

Run time 1h 18mins

Trivia

Audrey Hepburn (Chiquita) was considered for a larger role in this movie, but stage work made her unavailable. Sir Alec Guinness was impressed with the young actress and arranged for her to appear in a bit part. This is considered to be Hepburn's first appearance in a major movie.

Ealing Studios, planning a bank robbery movie, asked the Bank of England to devise a way in which a million pounds sterling could be stolen from the bank. A special committee was created to come up with an idea, and their plan is the one used in this movie.

Sir Alec Guinness was paid six thousand pounds sterling. His regular salary at this time was twenty-five thousand pounds sterling.

T.E.B. Clarke was originally meant to do a sequel to the popular police drama, The Blue Lamp (1950), but he quickly decided he'd much rather write a comedy instead.

Goofs

Stanley Holloway's voice in the gold-melting scene sounds as if it had been dubbed by another actor, and his lip movements in that scene don't quite match the sound of his voice.

During the chase, the license plate on the armoured truck is LKL238. The police officer correctly reports the license plate as LKL238. However, when the dispatcher repeats the license plate, he says LJL638.

The daily papers announcing the heist are dated 5th August 1950; however the evening paper, headlining the same news, is dated September.

MUSIC 1951

Artist	Single	Reached number one	Weeks at number one
1951			
Bing Crosby	Rudolph the Red-Nosed Reindeer	25th November 1950	6
Mel Blanc	I Taut I Taw a Puddy Tat	6th January 1951	3
Teddy Johnson	Beloved, Be Faithful	27th January 1951	1
Anne Shelton and Dick James	The Petite Waltz	3rd February 1951	2
Patti Page	Tennessee Waltz	17th February 1951	9
Les Paul and Mary Ford	Mockin' Bird Hill	21st April 1951	10
Jo Stafford and Nelson Eddy	With These Hands	30th June 1951	3
Hoagy Carmichael	My Resistance Is Low	21st July 1951	4
Jimmy Young	Too Young	18th August 1951	12
Teresa Brewer	Longing for You	10th November 1951	9

The cultural year was dominated by the Festival of Britain and the opening of The Royal Festival Hall, the first dedicated concert hall of its size to be built in London since 1893: located on the South bank of the Thames, this was to host concerts by major orchestras from Britain and abroad. The Festival itself was a celebration of music, art and theatre. It notably provided an opportunity for the staging of many events during the first Folk music Festival held in Edinburgh, organised with the help of such talents as the American Alan Lomax, the Irish traditional musician Seamus Ennis and the political theatre director Ewan MacColl, who would go on to form the Ballad and Blues Club.

The biggest selling artists on both sides of the Atlantic were Bing Crosby and Doris Day but British singers such as Gracie Fields and Vera Lynn were also very popular, receiving radio play and performing in many live venues.

Bing Crosby

" Rudolph the Red-Nosed Reindeer "

"Rudolph the Red-Nosed Reindeer" The song was first sung by crooner Harry Brannon on New York City radio in early November 1949, before Gene Autry's recording hit No. 1 in the U.S. charts during Christmas 1949. The song was suggested as a "B" side for a record Autry was making. Autry rejected the song. His wife convinced him to use it. The success of this Christmas song by Autry gave support to Autry's subsequent popular Easter song, "Here Comes Peter Cottontail."

The song was recorded by Bing Crosby on the 22nd June 1950 with John Scott Trotter and his Orchestra. Bing's song stayed at number one for 6 weeks in the United Kingdom

Mel Blanc

"I Taut I Taw a Puddy Tat"

"I Tawt I Taw A Puddy Tat" is a novelty song composed and written by Alan Livingston, Billy May and Warren Foster. It wa sung by Mel Blanc, who provided the voice of the bird, Tweet and of his nemesis Sylvester. The lyrics depict the basic formula of the Tweety-Sylvester cartoons released by Warner Bros. throughout the late 1940s into the early 1960s: Tweety wanting to live a contented life, only to be harassed by Sylvester (who is looking to eat the canary), and Tweety's mistress shooing the cat away. Toward the end of the song, t two perform a duet, with Tweety coaxing Sylvester into singir with him after promising that his (Tweety's) mistress won't chase him (Sylvester) away.

Mel Blanc stayed at number one for three weeks.

Teddy Johnson

"Beloved, Be Faithful"

"Beloved, Be Faithful" Edward Victor "Teddy" Johnson had led his own teenage band, was a professional drummer and a recording artist for Columbia in the early 1950s. He was also a DJ on Radio Luxembourg and later on BBC Radio 2, and had appeared in television shows such as the BBC's children's Crackerjack. Johnson and his wife Pearl Carr were frequently on British television light entertainment programmes, such as The Winifred Atwell Show as well as Big Night Out and Blackpool Night Out. They represented the United Kingdom in the Eurovision Song Contest 1959 and finished second with the song "Sing, Little Birdie". This peaked at No. 12 on the UK Singles Chart.

Teddy Johnson's song "Beloved, Be Faithful" went to number one for one week on the 27th January 1951.

Anne Shelton and Dick James

"The Petite Waltz"

"The Petite Waltz" Anne Shelton OBE born Patricia Jacqueline Sibley, was a popular English vocalist, who is remembered for providing inspirational songs for soldiers both on radio broadcasts, and in person, at British military bases during the Second World War.

Anna Shelton was also the original British singer of the Lale Anderson German love-song "Lili Marlene". Shelton appeared with Bing Crosby on the Variety Bandbox radio programme. In 1948 she recorded "If You Ever Fall in Love Again", wrote by Irish songwriter Dick Farrelly, who is best remembered for his song "Isle of Innisfree", which Shelton also recorded. Her songs "Galway Bay" and "Be Mine"

"The Petite Waltz " stayed at number one for two weeks on the 3rd February 1951.

Patti Page

"Tennessee Waltz"

"Tennessee Waltz" is a popular country music song with lyrics by Redd Stewart and music by Pee Wee King written in 1946 and first released in January 1948. The song became a multimillion seller via a 1950 recording – as "The Tennessee Waltz" – by Patti Page. Page cut "The Tennessee Waltz" in a November 1950 session in New York City with Rael conducting his orchestra: her vocal was cut multi-tracked with three voices, with two, and as a single voice with Page herself selecting the two-voice multi-tracked vocal featured on the single as released. "The Tennessee Waltz" entered the Pop Music chart of Billboard dated 10th November 1950 for a 30-week chart run and peaked at number one on the 17th February 1951.

The track would remain at number one for a total of nine weeks.

Les Paul and Mary Ford

"Mockin' Bird Hill"

" **Mockin' Bird Hill** " is a song written in 3/4 time by Carl "Calle" Jularbo, with lyrics by George Vaughn Horton and perhaps best known through recordings by Patti Page, Donna Fargo, and the duo of Les Paul and Mary Ford in 1951.

The first recording of "Mockin' Bird Hill" by an established act was made by Les Paul and Mary Ford, released as Capitol 1373 on the 29th January 1951. Les was one of the pioneers of the solid-body electric guitar, and his techniques served as inspiration for the Gibson Les Paul. Paul taught himself how to play guitar, and while he is mainly known for jazz and popular music, he had an early career in country music.

Mary Ford was an American vocalist and guitarist, comprising half of the husband-and-wife musical team Les Paul and Mary Ford. In 1951 alone they sold six million records.

Jo Stafford and Nelson Eddy

"With These Hands"

"With These Hands" is a song written by Benny Davis and Abner Silver. Jo Elizabeth Stafford was an American traditional pop music singer and occasional actress, whose career spanned five decades from the late 1930s to the early 1980s. Admired for the purity of her voice, she originally underwent classical training to become an opera singer before following a career in popular music, and by 1955 had achieved more worldwide record sales than any other female artist. Nelson Ackerman Eddy was an American singer, baritone and actor who appeared in 19 musical films during the 1930s and 1940s, as well as in opera and on the concert stage, radio, television, and in nightclubs and in his heyday, he was the highest paid singer in the world. There song "With These Hands" was number one for 3 weeks in the UK from the 30th June 1951.

Hoagy Carmichael

"My Resistance Is Low"

"My Resistance Is" Low is a 1951 song by American singer, songwriter and band leader Hoagy Carmichael, with later lyrics by Harold Adamson. Hoagland Howard "Hoagy" Carmichael was an American singer, songwriter, and actor. American composer and author Alec Wilder described Carmichael as the "most talented, inventive, sophisticated and jazz-oriented of all the great craftsmen" of pop songs in the first half of the 20th century. Carmichael was one of the most successful Tin Pan Alley songwriters of the 1930s and was among the first singer-songwriters in the age of mass media to utilize new communication technologies, such as television and the use of electronic microphones and sound recordings.

From July 21st for four weeks it made the number one spot in the charts.

Jimmy Young

"Too Young"

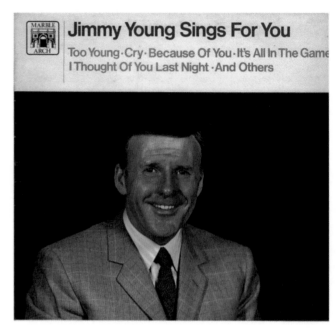

"Too Young" Jimmy Young signed to the new Polygon Records in 1950, joining Petula Clark, Louis Prima and Dorothy Squires. All his recordings on the label were conducted by Ron Goodwin. Goodwin later said he always liked working with Young "because he was always so enthusiastic. He thought everything we did was going to be a hit." The most popular was "Too Young" which he recorded in 1951, but this was before the days of UK record charts which didn't start until November 1952, so the record books do not list it. The song was a big sheet music seller at the time and was a cover version of the Nat King Cole original.

The song "Too Young" reached number one on the 28th August 1951 and stayed there for 12 weeks.

Teresa Brewer

"Longing for You"

"Longing for You" Teresa Brewer born Theresa Veronica Breuer was an American singer whose style incorporated pop, country, jazz, R&B, musicals, and novelty songs. She was one of the most prolific and popular female singers of the 1950s, recording nearly 600 songs. In 1949 she recorded the song Copenhagen (a jazz perennial) with the Dixieland All-Stars. For the B side she recorded the song "Music! Music! Music!". Unexpectedly, it was not the A side but the B side which took off, selling over a million copies and becoming Teresa's signature song. Another novelty song, "Choo'n Gum", hit the top 20 in 1950, followed by "Molasses, Molasses". Although she preferred to sing ballads, her only recorded ballad to make the charts was "Longing for You" in 1951. It reached number one on the 10th November 1951 and stayed there for 9 weeks.

WORLD EVENTS 1951

January

1st — Patti Page's hit song "Tennessee Waltz" enjoys its first week as the No. 1 single, on Billboard and Cashbox charts, in the United States.

The 50th anniversary of Australian federation is celebrated.

4th — Korean War: Third Battle of Seoul: Chinese and North Korean forces capture Seoul for the second time (they had lost Seoul in the Second Battle of Seoul in September 1950).

9th — The Government of the United Kingdom announces abandonment of the Tanganyika groundnut scheme for the cultivation of peanuts in the Tanganyika Territory, with the writing off of £36.5M debt.

15th — In a court in West Germany, Ilse Koch, The "Witch of Buchenwald", wife of the commandant of the Buchenwald concentration camp, is sentenced to life imprisonment. After the trial received worldwide media attention, survivor accounts of her actions resulted in other authors describing her abuse of prisoners as sadistic, and the image of her as "the concentration camp murderess" was current in post-war German society.

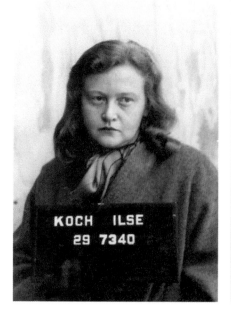 

20th — Avalanches in the Alps kill 240 and bury 45,000 for a time, in Switzerland, Austria and Italy.

25th — Dutch author Anne de Vries releases the first volume of her novel Journey Through the Night (Reis door de nacht), set during World War II.

27th — Nuclear testing at the Nevada Test Site begins, with a 1-kiloton bomb dropped on Frenchman Flat, northwest of Las Vegas.

31st — The United States' last narrow gauge passenger train (the "San Juan Express") ends service.

February

1st | The United Nations General Assembly declares that China is an aggressor in the Korean War, in United Nations General Assembly Resolution 498.

4th | Surgeons remove an ovarian cyst from Gertrude Levandowski in a 96-hour-long operation in Chicago. She loses almost half of her weight and emerges weighing 140 kg.

6th | The Woodbridge train derailment occurred on February 6, 1951 in Woodbridge, New Jersey, when a train derailed crossing a temporary wooden trestle, killing 86 people. In addition to being the deadliest train wreck in New Jersey, it is also the deadliest rail disaster in peacetime United States.

13th | The 1951 New Zealand waterfront dispute was the largest and most widespread industrial dispute in New Zealand history. During the time, up to twenty thousand workers went on strike in support of waterfront workers protesting against financial hardships and poor working conditions. Thousands more refused to handle "scab" goods. The dispute, sometimes referred to as the waterfront lockout or waterfront strike, lasted 151 days—from 13th February to the 15th July 1951.

19th | Jean Lee becomes the last woman hanged in Australia, when Lee and her 2 pimps are hanged for the murder and torture of a 73-year-old bookmaker.

25th | The 1951 Pan American Games (the I Pan American Games) were held in Buenos Aires, Argentina between February 25 and March 9, 1951. The Pan American Games' origins were at the Games of the X Olympiad in Los Angeles, United States, where officials representing the National Olympic Committees of the Americas discussed the staging of an Olympic-style regional athletic competition for the athletes of the Americas.

During the Pan-American Exposition at Dallas in 1937, a limited sports program was staged. These include Athletics, Boxing, and Wrestling among others. This program was considered a success and a meeting of Olympic officials from the Americas was held.

At the Pan American Sports Conference held in 1940, it was decided to hold the 1st Pan American Games at Buenos Aires, Argentina, in 1942. The Pan American Sports Committee was formed to govern the games. Avery Brundage was elected as the first President. However, the Japanese attack on Pearl Harbour brought much of the Americas into World War II, thus forcing the cancellation of the 1942 games.

A second conference was held in 1948. Avery Brundage was re-elected as the President of the PASC. It was decided that Buenos Aires would still host the 1st Pan American Games, this time in 1951.

27th | The Twenty-second Amendment to the United States Constitution sets a limit on the number of times an individual is eligible for election to the office of President of the United States, and also sets additional eligibility conditions for presidents who succeed to the unexpired terms of their predecessors. Prior to the ratification of the amendment, the president had not been subject to term limits, but George Washington had established a two-term tradition that many other presidents had followed. In the 1940 presidential election and the 1944 presidential election, Franklin D. Roosevelt became the first president to win a third term and then later a fourth term, giving rise to concerns about the potential issues involved with a president serving an unlimited number of terms. Congress approved the Twenty-second Amendment on March 24th 1947, and submitted it to the state legislatures for ratification. That process was completed on February 27th 1951, after the amendment had been ratified by the requisite 36 of the then-48 states and its provisions came into force on that date.

2nd The National Basketball Association All-Star Game is a basketball exhibition game hosted every February by the National Basketball Association (NBA) and showcases 24 of the league's star players. It is the featured event of NBA All-Star Weekend, a three-day event which goes from Friday to Sunday. The All-Star Game was first played at the Boston Garden on the 2nd March 1951.

3rd "Rocket 88" (originally written as Rocket "88") is a rhythm and blues song that was first recorded in Memphis, Tennessee, on the 3rd March 1951. The recording was credited to Jackie Brenston and his Delta Cats, who were actually Ike Turner and his Kings of Rhythm. "Rocket 88" reached number one on the Billboard R&B chart. Many music writers acknowledge its importance in the development of rock and roll music, with several considering it to be the first rock and roll record. The song was inducted into the Blues Hall of Fame in 1991, the Grammy Hall of Fame in 1998, and the Rock and Roll Hall of Fame Singles in 2018

6th The trial of Julius and Ethel Rosenberg for conspiracy to commit espionage begins in the United States.

9th The Man from Planet X was released on the 9th March 1951. It was an Independently made American black-and-white science fiction horror film, produced by Jack Pollexfen and Aubrey Wisberg, directed by Edgar G. Ulmer that stars Robert Clarke, Margaret Field, and William Schallert.

12th Dennis the Menace is a daily syndicated newspaper comic strip originally created, written, and illustrated by Hank Ketcham. It debuted on the 12th March 1951, in 16 newspapers and was originally distributed by Post-Hall Syndicate.

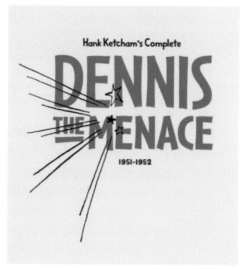

14th Operation Ripper was preceded by the largest artillery bombardment of the Korean War. On the middle, the US 25th Infantry Division quickly crossed the Han and established a bridgehead. Further to the east, IX Corps reached its first phase line on the 11th March. Three days later the advance proceeded to the next phase line. During the night of the 14th–15th March, elements of the ROK 1st Infantry Division and the US 3rd Infantry Division liberated Seoul, marking the fourth and last time the capital changed hands since June 1950. The PVA/KPA forces were compelled to abandon it when the UN approach to the east of the city threatened them with encirclement.

West Germany joins UNESCO.

March

29th | On March 29th 1951, the Rosenbergs were convicted of espionage. They were sentenced to death on the 5th April under Section 2 of the Espionage Act of 1917, which provides that anyone convicted of transmitting or attempting to transmit to a foreign government "information relating to the national defence" may be imprisoned for life or put to death.

Rodgers and Hammerstein's The King and I opens' on Broadway, and runs for three years. It is the first of their musicals specifically written for an actress (Gertrude Lawrence). Lawrence is stricken with cancer during the run of the show, and dies halfway through its run a year later. The show makes a star of Yul Brynner.

The 23rd Academy Awards Ceremony is held; All About Eve wins the Best Picture award and five others.

31st | The first Univac was accepted by the United States Census Bureau on the 31st March 1951, and was dedicated on June 14th that year. The fifth machine (built for the U.S. Atomic Energy Commission) was used by CBS to predict the result of the 1952 presidential election. With a sample of just 1% of the voting population it famously predicted an Eisenhower landslide. The UNIVAC I (UNIVersal Automatic Computer was the first general purpose electronic digital computer design for business application produced in the United States. It was designed principally by J. Presper Eckert and John Mauchly, the inventors of the ENIAC. ENIAC (Electronic Numerical Integrator and Computer) was the first electronic general-purpose computer. It was Turing-complete, digital and able to solve "a large class of numerical problems" through reprogramming.

April

5th | The most complete recording of George Gershwin's opera Porgy and Bess.

7th | Operation Greenhouse: The first thermonuclear burn is carried out on Enewetak Atoll in the Marshall Islands of the Pacific by the U.S. Three further tests in this series take place up to May 24.

11th | U.S. President Harry S. Truman relieves General Douglas MacArthur of his Far Eastern commands.

11th After its removal from Westminster Abbey on Christmas Day, 1950, the Stone of Scone resurfaces on the altar of Arbroath Abbey. The Stone of Scone—also known as the Stone of Destiny, and often referred to in England as The Coronation Stone—is an oblong block of red sandstone that has been used for centuries in the coronation of the monarchs of Scotland, and later also when the monarchs of Scotland became monarchs of England as well as in the coronations of the monarchs of Great Britain and latterly of the United Kingdom following the acts of union. Historically, the artefact was kept at the now-ruined Scone Abbey in Scone, near Perth, Scotland. It is also known as Jacob's Pillow Stone and the Tanist Stone, and in Scottish Gaelic, clach-na-cinneamhain. Its size is 66 cm (26 in) by 42.5 cm (16.7 in) by 26.7 cm (10.5 in) and its weight is approximately 152 kg (335 lb). A roughly incised cross is on one surface, and an iron ring at each end aids with transport. The Stone of Scone was last used in 1953 for the coronation of Elizabeth II of the United Kingdom of Great Britain and Northern Ireland.

18th The Treaty of Paris (formally the Treaty establishing the European Coal and Steel Community) was signed on the 18th April 1951 between France, West Germany, Italy and the three Benelux countries (Belgium, Luxembourg, and the Netherlands), establishing the European Coal and Steel Community, which subsequently became part of the European Union. The treaty came into force on the 23rd July 1952 and expired on the 23rd July 2002, exactly fifty years after it came into effect. The treaty was seen as producing diplomatic and economic stability in western Europe after the Second World War. Some of the main enemies during the war were now sharing production of coal and steel, the key-resources which previously had been central to the war effort.

21st The National Olympic Committee of the Soviet Union is formed. The USSR will first participate in the Olympic Games at Helsinki, Finland, in 1952.

24th In Yokohama, Japan, a fire on a train kills more than 100.

28th The 1951 Australian federal election was held in Australia on the 28th April 1951. All 121 seats in the House of Representatives and all 60 seats in the Senate were up for election, due to a double dissolution called after the Senate rejected the Commonwealth Bank Bill. The incumbent Liberal–Country coalition led by Prime Minister Robert Menzies defeated the opposition Labor Party led by Ben Chifley with a modestly reduced majority, and secured a majority in the Senate. This was the last time the Labor party ever held a Senate majority. Chifley died just over a month after the election.

May

1st | The opera house of Geneva, Switzerland is almost destroyed in a fire.

3rd | King George VI opens London's Royal Festival Hall as a patron.

The U.S. Senate Committee on Armed Services and U.S. Senate Committee on Foreign Relations begin their closed door hearings into the dismissal of General Douglas MacArthur, by U.S. President Harry S Truman.

9th | Operation Greenhouse: The first thermonuclear weapon is tested on Enewetok Atoll in the Marshall Islands, by the United States.

14th | The Talyllyn Railway is a narrow gauge preserved railway in Wales running for 7 1/4 miles (12 km) from Tywyn on the Mid-Wales coast to Nant Gwernol near the village of Abergynolwyn. The line was opened in 1865 to carry slate from the quarries at Bryn Eglwys to Tywyn, and was the first narrow gauge railway in Britain authorised by Act of Parliament to carry passengers using steam haulage. Despite severe under-investment, the line remained open, and on the 14th May 1951 it became the first railway in the world to be preserved as a heritage railway by volunteers.

15th | A military coup occurs in Bolivia.

21st | The 9th Street Art Exhibition, otherwise known as the 9th St. Show or Ninth Street Show was held on May 21st -June 10th 1951. This was a historical, ground-breaking exhibition, gathering of a number of notable artists, and it was the stepping-out of the post war New York avant-garde, collectively known as the New York School. The show was hung by Leo Castelli, as he was liked by most of the artists and thought of as someone who would hang the exhibition without favouritism. The opening of the show was a great success. According to the critic, historian, and curator Bruce Altshuler, "It appeared as though a line had been crossed, a step into a larger art world whose future was bright with possibility."

23rd | The Tibetan government signs the Seventeen Point Agreement for the Peaceful Liberation of Tibet, with the People's Republic of China.

25th | The first atomic bomb "boosted" by the inclusion of thermonuclear materials, is tested in the "Item" test on Enewetok Atoll in the Marshall Islands by the United States.

28th | The Goon Show was a British radio comedy programme, originally produced and broadcast by the BBC Home Service from 1951 to 1960, with occasional repeats on the BBC Light Programme. The first series, broadcast from the 28th May to the 20th September 1951, was titled Crazy People; subsequent series had the title The Goon Show, a title inspired, according to Spike Milligan, by a Popeye character.

The show's chief creator and main writer was Spike Milligan. The scripts mixed ludicrous plots with surreal humour, puns, catchphrases and an array of bizarre sound effects. Some of the later episodes feature electronic effects devised by the fledgling BBC Radiophonic Workshop, many of which were reused by other shows for decades. Many elements of the show satirised contemporary life in Britain, parodying aspects of show business, commerce, industry, art, politics, diplomacy, the police, the military, education, class structure, literature and film.

The show was released internationally through the BBC Transcription Services. It was heard regularly from the 1950s in Australia, South Africa, New Zealand, India, and Canada, although these TS versions were frequently edited to avoid controversial subjects. In the United States, NBC began broadcasting the programme on its radio network from the mid-1950s

 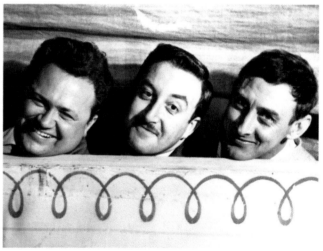

4th | The Foley Square trial concludes review in the U.S. Supreme Court as Dennis v. United States, with a ruling against the defendants (overturned by Yates v. United States in 1957).

15th | In New Mexico, Arizona, California, Oregon, Washington and British Columbia, thousands of hectares of forests are destroyed in fires.

Battle Ground, Washington is incorporated. Battle Ground got its name from a standoff between a group of the Klickitat peoples and a military force from the Vancouver Barracks, which had recently transitioned to a U.S. Army post. Battle Ground is located about 11 miles (18 km) north northeast of Vancouver, 32 miles (51 km) south southwest of Mount St. Helens.

June

1st | Judy Garland opens the first of 14 concerts in Dublin, Ireland at the Theatre Royal.

5th | William Shockley, John Bardeen and Walter Brattain announce the invention of the junction transistor.

10th | Korean War: Armistice negotiations begin at Kaesong.

A formal peace agreement between Canada and Germany is signed.

11th | The Cicero race riot of 1951 occurred on the 11th July 1951, when a mob of 4,000 whites attacked an apartment building that housed a single black family in a neighbourhood in Cicero, Illinois.

13th | On the 13th July 1951, heavy rains led to a great rise of water in the Kansas River and other surrounding areas of the central United States. Flooding resulted in the Kansas, Neosho, Marais Des Cygnes, and Verdigris river basins. The damage in June and July 1951 exceeded $935 million in an area covering easter Kansas and Missouri, which, adjusting for inflation, is nearly $8.52 billion in 2016. The flood resulted in th loss of 17 lives and displaced 518,000 people.

MGM's Technicolor film version of Show Boat, starring Kathryn Grayson, Ava Gardner, and Howard Keel, premieres at Radio City Music Hall in New York City. The musical brings overnight fame to African American bass-baritone William Warfield (who sings Ol' Man River in the film).

14th | In Diamond, Missouri, the George Washington Carver National Monument becomes the first United States National Monument to honour an African American.

16th | King Leopold III of Belgium abdicates, in favour of his son Baudouin.

17th | J. D. Salinger's coming-of-age story The Catcher in the Rye is published by Little, Brown and Company in New York City.

LITTLE, BROWN AND COMPANY

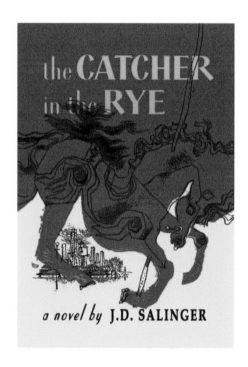

20th | King Abdullah I of Jordan is assassinated by a Palestinian, while attending Friday prayers in Jerusalem. He is succeeded by his son, King Talal.

26th | Walt Disney's 13th animated film, Alice in Wonderland, premieres in London, United Kingdom.

30th | David Lean's film of Oliver Twist is finally shown in the United States, after 10 minutes of supposedly anti-Semitic references and close-ups of Alec Guinness as Fagin are cut. It will not be shown uncut in the U.S. until 1970.

August

11th | René Pleven becomes Prime Minister of France.

16th | The Australian Financial Review is first published.

31st | The first Volkswagen Type 1 rolls off the production line in Uitenhage, South Africa.

September

1st | The United States, Australia and New Zealand all sign a mutual defence pact, the ANZUS Treaty.

2nd | The Sri Lanka Freedom Party is founded by S. W. R. D. Bandaranaike.

3rd | The American soap opera Search for Tomorrow debuts on CBS. The show switches to NBC on March 26, 1982 and airs its final episode on December 26, 1986.

8th | The Treaty of San Francisco, also called the Treaty of Peace with Japan, re-established peaceful relations between Japan and the Allied Powers after World War II. It was officially signed by 49 nations on the 8th September 1951, in San Francisco, California at the War Memorial Opera House. It came into force on the 28th April 1952, and officially ended the American-led Allied occupation of Japan. According to Article 11 of the treaty, Japan accepts the judgments of the International Military Tribunal for the Far East and of other Allied War Crimes Courts imposed on Japan both within and outside Japan.

9th | Chinese Communist forces move into Lhasa, the capital of Tibet.

10th | The United Kingdom begins an economic boycott of Iran.

18th | Elia Kazan's adaptation of the Tennessee Williams play A Streetcar Named Desire premieres, becoming a critical and box-office smash.

20th | NATO accepts Greece and Turkey as members.

26th | A blue sun is seen over Europe: the effect is due to ash coming from the Canadian forest fires 4 months previously.

28th | 20th Century Fox releases the Robert Wise science fiction film The Day the Earth Stood Still in the United States.

30th | Charlotte Whitton becomes mayor of Ottawa and Canada's first woman mayor of a major city.

3rd | "Shot Heard 'Round the World (baseball)": One of the greatest moments in Major League Baseball history occurs when the New York Giants' Bobby Thomson hits a game-winning home run in the bottom of the 9th inning off of Brooklyn Dodgers pitcher Ralph Branca, to win the National League pennant after being down 14 games.

The First Battle of Maryang-san (3–8 October 1951), also known as the Defensive Battle of Maliangshan Pinyin, was fought during the Korean War between United Nations Command (UN) forces—primarily Australian and British—and the Chinese People's Volunteer Army (PVA). The fighting occurred during a limited UN offensive by US I Corps, codenamed Operation Commando. This offensive ultimately pushed the PVA back from the Imjin River to the Jamestown Line and destroyed elements of four PVA armies following heavy fighting. The much smaller battle at Maryang San took place over a five-day period, and saw the 3rd Battalion, Royal Australian Regiment (3 RAR) dislodge a numerically superior PVA force from the tactically important Kowang san (Hill 355) and Maryang san (Hill 317) features, in conjunction with other units of the 1st Commonwealth Division.

Using tactics first developed against the Japanese in New Guinea during the Second World War, the Australians gained the advantage of the high ground and assaulted the PVA positions from unexpected directions. They then repelled repeated PVA counterattacks aimed at re-capturing Maryang San, with both sides suffering heavy casualties before the Australians were finally relieved by a British battalion. However, with the peace-talks ongoing, these operations proved to be the last actions in the war of manoeuvre, which had lasted the previous sixteen months. It was replaced by a static war characterised by fixed defences reminiscent of the Western Front in 1915–17. A month later, the PVA re-captured Maryang San during fierce fighting, and it was never re-gained. Today, the battle is widely regarded as one of the Australian Army's greatest accomplishments during the war.

4th | MGM's Technicolor musical film, An American in Paris, starring Gene Kelly and Leslie Caron, and directed by Vincente Minnelli, premieres in New York. It will go on to win 6 Academy Awards, including Best Picture.

6th | Malayan Emergency: Communist insurgents kill British commander Sir Henry Gurney.

10th | The New York Yankees defeat the New York Giants (baseball), 4 games to 2, to win the 14th World Series Title.

October

14th | THE Organization of Central American States (Organización de Estados Centroamericanos, ODECA) is formed.

15th | Norethisterone, the progestin used in the combined oral contraceptive pill, is synthesized by Luis E. Miramontes in Mexico.

I Love Lucy, the American television sitcom started on CBS from the 15th October 1951, to the 6th May 1957, with a total of 180 half-hour episodes spanning 6 seasons (including the 'lost' original pilot and Christmas episode). The show starred Lucille Ball, her real-life husband Desi Arnaz, Vivian Vance, and William Frawley. It followed the life of Lucy Ricardo (Ball), a middle class housewife in New York City, who either concocted plans with her best friends (Vance & Frawley) to appear alongside her bandleader husband Ricky Ricardo (Arnaz) in his nightclub, or tried numerous schemes to mingle with, or be a part of show business.

16th | Judy Garland begins a series of concerts in New York's Palace Theatre.

17th | CBS's Eye logo premieres on American television.

19th | The state of war between the United States and Germany is officially ended.

20th | The Johnny Bright incident was a violent on-field assault against African-American player Johnny Bright by a white opposing player during an American college football game held on the 20th October 1951, in Stillwater, Oklahoma. The game was significant in itself as it marked the first time that an African-American athlete with a national profile and of critical importance to the success of his team, the Drake Bulldogs, had played against Oklahoma A&M College (now Oklahoma State University) at Oklahoma A&M's Lewis Field. Bright's injury also highlighted the racial tensions of the times and assumed notoriety when it was captured in what was later to become both a widely disseminated and eventually Pulitzer Prize-winning photo sequence.

21st | A storm in southern Italy kills over 100.

26th | Winston Churchill is re-elected Prime Minister of the United Kingdom (a month before his 77th birthday) a general election which sees the defeat of Clement Attlee's Labour government, after 6 years in power.

27th | Farouk of Egypt declares himself king of Sudan, with no support.

28th | The town of Carnation, Washington, USA changes its name back to Carnation, after being named Tolt since May 1928.

31st | The film Scrooge, starring Alastair Sim, opens in England.

November

1st | The first military exercises for nuclear war, with infantry troops included, are held in the Nevada desert.

2nd | 6,000 British troops flown into Egypt to quell unrest in the Suez Canal zone

November

10th	Direct dial coast-to-coast telephone service begins in North America.
11th	Monogram Pictures releases the sci-fi film Flight to Mars in the United States.
12th	The National Ballet of Canada performs for the first time in Eaton Auditorium, Toronto.
20th	The Po River floods in northern Italy.
22nd	Paramount Pictures releases the George Pal science fiction film When Worlds Collide in the United States.
24th	The Broadway play Gigi opens, starring little known actress Audrey Hepburn as the lead character.

28th	The U.K. film Scrooge, starring Alastair Sim, premieres in the United States under the title of Charles Dickens's original novel, A Christmas Carol.
29th	The LEO I (Lyons electronic office I) was the first computer used for commercial business applications.

The prototype LEO I was modelled closely on the Cambridge EDSAC. Its construction was overseen by Oliver Standingford, Raymond Thompson and David Caminer of J. Lyons and Co. LEO I ran its first business application on November 29th 1951. In 1954 Lyons formed LEO Computers Ltd to market LEO I and its successors LEO II and LEO III to other companies. LEO Computers eventually became part of English Electric Company (EELM) where the same team developed the faster LEO 360 and even faster LEO 326 models. It then passed to International Computers Limited (ICL) and ultimately Fujitsu.

December

1st | The Institute of War and Peace Studies is established by Dwight D. Eisenhower at Columbia University in New York (of which he is President) with William T. R. Fox as first director.

3rd | Lebanese University is founded in Lebanon.

5th | The Provisional Intergovernmental Committee for the Movement of Migrants from Europe is formed.

6th | A state of emergency is declared in Egypt, due to increasing riots.

13th | A water storage tank collapses in Tucumcari, New Mexico, resulting in 4 deaths and 200 buildings destroyed.

16th | The Salar Jung Museum is opened to the public, by Prime Minister of India Jawaharlal Nehru.

17th | We Charge Genocide, a petition describing genocide against African Americans, are delivered to the United Nations.

20th | Experimental Breeder Reactor I (EBR-I) is a decommissioned research reactor and U.S. National Historic Landmark located in the desert about 18 miles (29 km) southeast of Arco, Idaho. It was the world's first breeder reactor. At 1:50 p.m. on the 20th December 1951, it became one of the world's first electricity-generating nuclear power plants when it produced sufficient electricity to illuminate four 200-watt light bulbs. Electricity had earlier been generated by a nuclear reactor on September 3, 1948 at the X-10 Graphite Reactor in Oak Ridge, Tennessee. EBR-I subsequently generated sufficient electricity to power its building, and continued to be used for experimental purposes until it was decommissioned in 1964. The museum is open for visitors from late May until early September.

A chartered Curtiss C-46 Commando crash-lands in Cobourg, Ontario Canada; all on board survive.

The World Meteorological Organization becomes a specialized agency of the United Nations.

22nd | The Selangor Labour Party is founded in Selangor, Malaya.

24th | Gian Carlo Menotti's 45-minute opera, Amahl and the Night Visitors, premieres live on NBC in the United States, becoming the first opera written especially for television.

Libya becomes independent from Italy; Idris I is proclaimed King.

31st | The Marshall Plan expires, after distributing more than $13.3 billion US in foreign aid to rebuild Europe.

PEOPLE IN POWER

Robert Menzies
1949-1966
Australia
Prime Minister

Vincent Auriol
1947-1954
France
Président

Eurico Gaspar Dutra
1946-1951
Brazil
President

Louis St. Laurent
1948-1957
Canada
Prime Minister

Mao Zedong
1943-1976
China
Government of China

Theodor Heuss
1949-1959
Germany
President of Germany

Rajendra Prasad
1950-1962
India
1st President of India

Luigi Einaudi
1948-1955
Italy
President

Hiroito
1926-1989
Japan
Emperor

Miguel Alemán Valdés
1946-1952
Mexico
46th President of Mexico

Joseph Stalin
1922-1952
Russia
Premier

D. F. Malan
1948-1954
South Africa
Prime Minister

Harry S. Truman
1945-1953
United States
President

Joseph Pholien
1950-1952
Belgium
Prime Minister

Sidney Holland
1949-1957
New Zealand
Prime Minister

Sir Winston Churchill
1951-1955
United Kingdom
Prime Minister

Tage Erlander
1946-1969
Sweden
Prime Minister

Erik Eriksen
1950-1953
Denmark
Prime Minister

Francisco Franco
1936-1975
Spain
President

Mátyás Rákosi
1948-1956
Hungary
Hungarian Working
People's Party

The Year You Were Born 1951
Book by Sapphire Publishing

Printed in Great Britain
by Amazon